SURVIVING DIVORCE

A Handbook for Men

By the same author

Divorce and After (1979)
The Down Your Way Book (1980)
Hit Back! (with Chris Biffen) (1983)
Variations on Wayne Sleep (1983)

SURVIVING DIVORCE

A Handbook for Men

Gay Search

Elm Tree Books London

First published in Great Britain 1983
by Elm Tree Books Ltd
Garden House, 57–59 Long Acre, London WC2E 9JZ

Published in the United States of America by
Elm Tree Books in association with
David & Charles Inc, North Pomfret, Vermont 05053, USA

ISBN 0–241–10954–X

Photoset in Great Britain by
Rowland Phototypesetting Ltd
Bury St Edmunds, Suffolk

Printed in Great Britain by Billings, Worcester

Contents

Introduction

The idea for this book grew from a magazine article I wrote five years ago on the plight of the divorced father. What struck me most forcibly was the number of men who simply had no idea when their divorce began, of what was going to happen. Most of them had no experience of divorce, but because they had always believed British justice to be the finest in the world, they had somehow assumed that the outcome would be fair. The realisation that, all too often, it wasn't was devastating, and by the time it dawned, it was too late to do anything about it.

Surviving Divorce: A Handbook for Men sets out to tell any man on the brink of divorce what the outcome is likely to be for himself, his children, his home and his financial position, and what he can do to mitigate the most damaging effects.

I am not for one moment claiming that men are always the victims in divorce. Some men do behave extremely badly and irresponsibly, but so do some women, and unfortunately the legal system doesn't encourage them to behave any better. But when men are also fathers, divorce all too often relegates them to the sidelines of their children's lives, or excludes them altogether, and since its been shown that children need a relationship with both their natural parents, *they* are the real victims.

Divorce is never an easy way out, even if it is the only way out, but with some foreknowledge, it's possible to survive it intact.

G.S. 1983

Acknowledgements

Grateful thanks to the many men and women who shared their expertise and experience with me.
I and my publishers would also like to thank Jill Norman & Hobhouse for permission to quote from *I'm Leaving* by Bente and Gunnar Oberg and George Allen & Unwin for permission to quote from *Divorce and Your Money* by W. Harper.

For Tony
in the hope he never needs it

1

Marriages in Trouble

Divorce in Britain today is reaching epidemic proportions. One in three marriages now end in divorce, and though most people do marry again, the failure rate for second marriages is even higher. We have the highest divorce rate in Europe, and though we're not yet in the same league as the United States where slightly more than one marriage in two now ends in divorce so the odds of your staying married are now against you, the way we're going, we soon will be.

The reasons why people divorce are as complex and as confused as the reasons why they get married in the first place, and there is no *simple* explanation for the sharp rise in the number of divorces in the last ten years or so.

Certainly the change in the law in 1969, which made divorce easier, has had something to do with it. As expected, the provision which allowed people to get divorced *without* their partner's consent if they had lived apart for five years or more, did create a 'bulge' in the early seventies, as thousands of people who had been trapped in dead marriages for years were able to end them legally. But even allowing for that 'bulge', the divorce figures have gone on rising – from approximately 54,000 in 1968 to 109,000 in 1972 to 170,000 in 1981.

Some people blame easier divorce for the increased number of marriages that break down, but if that were true, then a country like the Irish Republic which has no divorce at all should also have no broken marriages, which, of course, just isn't the case. Equally, no-one knows how many people were forced to stay in failed marriages before the law was changed because there was no alternative. Many women would not have been able to support themselves or their children if they left home, and besides, the social stigma attached to divorce was so much stronger then, and could actually prevent people from getting work, or housing.

But if more liberal divorce laws don't actually cause marriages to break down, it would be true to say that now divorce is so widespread and easy, many couples assume, when their marriage hits a bad patch, that it is the only answer. Divorce has become the first resort, not the last.

A survey carried out by *Woman* magazine in the spring of 1982, suggests that for many people it is a case of 'divorce in haste, repent at leisure.' Of all the divorced people interviewed, one in three said they wished they had tried harder to save the marriage – men even more so than women.

It is tempting to see divorce as the answer to all your problems, but it very rarely is. Maybe the root of your problems isn't your marriage at all. Perhaps you've been having a very difficult, stressful time at work, so you've become preoccupied at home, irritable with your wife and children, not interested in sex. Perhaps you've been unemployed for some time, and the frustration, the feeling of hopelessness and inadequacy have undermined your self-confidence to such an extent that you don't feel you have a role in the family any more.

It's not uncommon to find people thinking about divorce after some major emotional crisis in their lives – a serious illness, perhaps, or the death of a parent, or very close friend. It's as though your whole life feels wrong, which results in tension at home, and rows with your wife, so that you assume the marriage is the cause of all your difficulties. Once you're out of it, you tell yourself, everything will be all right again.

Some people only look as far ahead as the divorce itself, forgetting that divorce is not an event, but a process, and simply don't think about what their life will be like afterwards.

You may well lose your children to all intents and purposes, you will probably lose your home and you will certainly be poorer – so poor in fact that you may not be able to afford to remarry and start a second family, which means you may be intensely lonely.

But this isn't a plea to stay in a bad marriage, either for the sake of the children, or simply because the alternatives are too frightening. It's more a plea to be absolutely certain that yours *is* a bad marriage, with no hope for the future, rather than a marriage which has hit a very bad patch, and to explore all the possibilities before deciding that divorce is the only answer.

When you are having real problems with your marriage, there is a danger that you'll believe that once it's gone wrong, it can never come right again, or see your relationship, as Katherine Whitehorn has put it, as 'a flame that has blown out, not a fire that might need stoking.'

Even when divorce is the right thing to do, and even when you will be happier and more fulfilled as a result, it will cause a lot of unhappiness for your children, and will be probably the most traumatic experience of your adult life. Painless divorce just doesn't exist. So before you decide finally that divorce is the answer, it is worth exploring all the possibilities. Admittedly, many men find it extremely difficult to seek help with anything as personal and as sensitive as a problem with their marriage – counselling agencies get at least twice as many women clients as men.

You may be reluctant to seek help because you believe that once you admit to anyone that you have problems, then the marriage is definitely over, or that you are both adults and ought to be able to sort it out between you without any outside 'interference'. You may have been brought up to believe that 'big boys don't cry', and to see any display of emotion as an embarrassing display of weakness. Or you may simply find it extremely difficult to put your feelings into words.

Do remember that counsellors are trained to help you express your feelings, and that they deal with people's most intimate, painful personal problems all the time, so that nothing you say will shock or alarm them.

But don't expect miracles. Counselling won't solve all your problems for you, or make decisions, but what it can do is help you recognise what the problems are, acknowledge your part in them and see your wife's point of view. In the light of that, you will be in a much better position to make decisions about the future.

So, where can you go for help if you are having problems with your marriage?

Marriage Guidance Councils

In most big towns, there is a Marriage Guidance Council, staffed by volunteers who have all gone through pretty rigorous screening, and a two-year training programme. Their approach is not to give advice, or tell you what you ought to do, but to give you 'insight' – in other words, to help you to see for yourself what the difficulties are and the best way to resolve them.

They will see you and your wife separately or together, and if your wife refuses to go, they will see you on your own.

Marriage guidance, on the whole, is long-term, rather than short-term, and the process takes months rather than weeks. As one experienced counsellor put it, 'The client who comes to us thinking that we're rather like a doctor who will be able to give them a prescription on their first visit which will cure their ailing marriage, is going to be disappointed.'

Ron and his wife Jean spent an hour a week with their counsellor over a six-month period. 'At first we used to quarrel after the sessions – "Why did you have to say that in front of her?" – but gradually I found my eyes being opened. At first, I just couldn't believe that there was anything wrong with our marriage, but I began to see that I was at least partly to blame. I used to do a lot of work in the evenings to make extra money for Jean and the kids, but being on her own so much got Jean down, and she was afraid to talk to me about it because I'd shout at her.

'We hadn't been able to talk things over on our own, but in front of a neutral third party, it was easier somehow. The sessions would clear the air, and if we found ourselves getting into a row, we'd say, "Let's leave it till Tuesday evening," instead of rowing in front of the children like we used to.'

Even though his marriage ended two years later, Ron feels that marriage guidance was extremely valuable. 'When we did split up finally, at least I could see why it had to happen, and I think we were able to part with much less bitterness and anger than there would have been otherwise – on my side at least.'

But of course, marriage guidance doesn't work for everyone. John and his wife, for instance, tried two different counsellors before abandoning the idea. 'With the first one, there was basically a personality clash, and though the second one was better, I found that their general approach wasn't particularly helpful. There was too much listening. I wished they had sometimes ventured an opinion of their own – even if was only to say, "Don't be so stupid!" You do need that at times.'

At least John gave marriage guidance a try before rejecting it.

A lot of people don't even get that far. They're put off by its image – middle-class 'ladies-in-hats', trying to patch up dead marriages. Renate Olins of the London Marriage Guidance Council accepts that most of their counsellors are middle-class – 'So are doctors, social workers and so on, and when you rely wholly on volunteers, as we do, you find that they are the people who have the time to spare' – but she fiercely rejects the rest of it. 'What we offer is help with personal relationships in all their infinite variety, and at any stage. We will not push people into staying married, not will we hurry them towards divorce. What we aim to do is simply help them decide what is the best course of action for them.'

One practical problem with marriage guidance is that some Councils have long waiting lists, which is not ideal if you have reached breaking point, though if it is a real emergency, they might be able to see you more quickly. They don't charge, but they do ask for a contribution according to your means. With all the local authority cut-backs, though, some Marriage Guidance Councils are losing their grants, so they are having to rely more and more on contributions to cover their overheads.

The Catholic Marriage Advisory Council, and the Jewish Marriage Education Council offer help and counselling within a religious framework (see page 151 for addresses).

The Probation Service

You may not realise that probation officers, particularly those who work in the divorce courts as divorce court welfare officers, have a lot of experience in dealing with marriage problems, and may be able to help you. A lot of people are put off because they associate probation officers with the courts and crime, but their marriage advisory work is quite separate and any help they give you is in the strictest confidence. They will probably be able to see you more quickly than Marriage Guidance and there is no charge.

National Council for the Divorced and Separated Divorce Counselling Centres

Although as their name suggests, they concentrate mainly on the problems of divorce, they will see people who are thinking about divorce, though their approach is short-term rather than long-term (see page 151).

The Samaritans

If you are really desperate, and can't get help anywhere else, you can always ring the Samaritans (dial 100 and ask the operator for the number of the nearest centre). They will be prepared to talk to you for as long as you need and as often, though they may well recommend that you contact Marriage Guidance. If there is a delay in getting an appointment, then the Samaritans can provide an invaluable stop-gap service.

If you live in or near London, the Institute of Marital Studies at the Tavistock Institute in Hampstead offers counselling. It involves a very deep examination of your attitudes and emotions, and requires a lot of commitment. You both have to attend the weekly sessions, which could go on for six months or even a year or more. The initial appointment costs £16.50, though if you're unemployed, it is free, and each of the subsequent appointments will cost what you can afford to pay, so that no-one is turned away simply because they can't afford the fees.

The Divorce and Conciliation Advisory Service in London also offers help to people who are thinking about divorce, by laying out all the pros and cons, and helping them to understand the reality of divorce. They charge £15 for the first consultation, and £10 a hour for subsequent visits, but again, if you are really hard up and can't get help elsewhere, they will charge you less, or even waive the fees altogether.

If you feel that the problems in your marriage stem from difficulties in your sexual relationship, it might be worth seeking specialist help. It is often quite difficult to decide whether your marriage is suffering because you're having sexual difficulties, or whether the sexual problems are the result of difficulties in your relationship. If it is the former, then many family planning clinics, some run by the Family Planning Association, but most run by the National Health Service, can offer help with psycho-sexual problems. Your family doctor will be able to tell you where the nearest clinic is, but if you find it rather embarrassing to ask him or her, the British Association for Counselling publish a directory of all organisations in the British Isles offering such help.

It may well be that counselling won't save your marriage, but in any case it will be time well spent. At least you will know that you have explored all the possibilities, and it could make the process of separation and ultimately divorce, just a bit less painful.

2

Separating

There seems little doubt that the temper of your divorce – whether it's good, bad, or even – and therefore of your relationship with your children afterwards, depends to a large extent on the way in which you and your wife separate. If it's done very suddenly, amid great anger and bitterness, then the chances of keeping the subsequent divorce civilised and free from conflict are much less good than if it's done after a lot of thought and with great care to minimise the damage done.

But of course, that isn't always possible if a crisis has lead to you separating, or if one of you has been working yourself up for months to the point where you can actually leave. In either case, separation will be a time of maximum emotional stress, when you are least able to make calm, rational decisions about the long-term future. And yet the decisions you do make at that time, simply by virtue of what you actually do, will have the most profound effect on several important areas of your future life.

Suppose you and your wife have reached the point where you can't go on as you are any longer, and separation is the only answer, so you agree that it will be easiest all round if you move out. Chances are you're thinking only of the immediate future, giving yourselves a breathing space so that you will be able to make long-term decisions – about the children's future and what happens to the family home – in a calmer, less stressful atmosphere.

But the very fact that you have moved out, *regardless of who is responsible for the intolerable situation that made it necessary*, will to a large extent dictate with which of you the children will live and who stays in the family home when the case comes to court. As far as your home is concerned, if you have no children and can't agree which of you should stay in it, then the court will usually allow whoever is living in it at the time of the hearing to stay, although if you own it, the one who stays will probably have to buy the other out.

If you move in with your family, a friend, or a girlfriend, the judge may well take the view when the case comes to court, that you already have somewhere to live, so you have less of a claim on the family home, or a share in it.

If you do have children, and you and your wife can't agree about who shall have custody, then as far as the court is concerned, the most important factor in deciding their future is the *status quo* at the time of the hearing – in other words, whoever is looking after the children when the case comes to court, will almost certainly be allowed to keep them.

If you have moved out, leaving the children with your wife, then you stand very little chance indeed of getting custody. If your wife was the one to go, however, she stands a better chance of getting custody, in spite of the *status quo* (see page 72).

In the vast majority of cases, whoever 'gets' the children, also gets the family home. If you own your home, then the court may well award you a share of its value (see page 100), but they will allow your wife to go on living there with the children until they have finished school, so there is no chance of you realising your share for some years, if at all. If you live in a rented house or flat, whether it's private or council, the court will order the tenancy to be transferred to whichever of you has custody of the children.

Recent research has shown that an increasing number of couples are still living under the same roof when they start divorce proceedings, which could mean that more people are becoming aware of the long-term consequences of moving out, or simply that it is so difficult to find reasonable accommodation these days that many people have no choice but to stay.

Being forced to stay under the same roof once you've decided your marriage is over can create terrible problems, especially if there is a lot of anger and bitterness between you. There is nothing you can do about it, but your wife can apply to the local magistrates' court, or county court for an exclusion order, or an 'ouster', which will force you to leave your home.

Applications for exclusion orders have become much more common since the introduction of the Domestic Violence and

Matrimonial Proceedings Act 1976. Its aim was to give much-needed protection to battered women and children, by ordering violent men not to assault their wives and/or children – a 'non-molestation order' – or to leave, and not re-enter the family home – an 'exclusion order'.

Originally, a woman had to be able to prove serious or repeated violence had taken place, or had been threatened before the courts would make an exclusion order, and in the magistrates' court, that is still the case. In the county courts, though, a number of cases in recent years have shown that it isn't always necessary to prove violence, or even the threat of violence for an exclusion order to be made – serious friction between you, which is distressing the children, can be enough. In one case there had been no physical violence, or threat of it, but the wife said that unless the husband left the house, she would leave and put the children into care, because she had nowhere else to take them. The court decided that in the interests of the children, the husband would have to leave, even though he had done nothing to warrant it.

Blame is more or less irrelevant, so it is possible for a wife to be largely responsible for the intolerable situation in the home, and yet still be able to get her husband excluded from it on the strength of it. As the law stands, it is possible for an unscrupulous wife to use an exclusion order to get her husband out of the home, and so establish a *status quo* which will be favourable to her when the case comes to court.

According to an experienced divorce court welfare officer, it has become too easy for women to get their husbands out of the family home. 'A lot of the applications I hear are very dodgy, based on half-truths, and I must say, it is often the case that the day after the husband is turfed out, the boyfriend moves in. I don't think men should be turfed out of their homes unless there is medical evidence that they have been violent.'

Jim and his wife agreed their marriage was over, but since neither of them wanted to remarry, there was no hurry for a divorce, and they decided to stay together till they could sort out the practicalities. 'We planned to sell the house, pay off the mortgage and buy a house outright for my wife and the children, so that I could then get a mortgage to buy myself a flat. But then, I was made redundant, which held things up for a while. Eventually, I got another job and in the first week I got a letter from my wife's solicitor saying she wanted to go ahead with the divorce. I was really angry, because the new job was very demanding, and I couldn't cope with all the domestic upheaval then as well. The result was a terrible row in which she pulled my hair and I slapped her face. Next thing I knew, I was served with an exclusion order, telling me to get out of the house. From that moment, any hope of our sorting it out in a reasonably civilised way went right out the window!'

Usually, applications for exclusion orders are made 'on notice', which means that you must be informed that your wife has made an application, and given a chance to put your side of the story in court, producing witnesses if you can.

On the other hand, if your wife can show that she and the children are in danger from you, she can make the application 'ex parte', which means that you are given no warning or opportunity to defend yourself, and the first you know about it is when you are served with the order by your wife's solicitors, if she has applied in the county court, or by a policeman if she applied in the magistrates' court.

Once the order has been served on you, there is little you can do but comply with it. If your wife is claiming that your mere presence in the home is causing stress which is harming the children, and can produce a letter from a doctor or the school to say that they are suffering, then even if you believe that it's your wife's behaviour that is causing the stress, the court will probably order you out of the home. If the order has the 'power of arrest' attached, then the police must arrest you if you disobey it. If there is no 'power of arrest' attached, then your wife can go back to court if you disobey it, and you could be arrested for contempt of court.

There are other, less dramatic and distressing ways of putting your decision to separate on a formal, legal footing, though whether or not you need to do so depends on what decisions you have made about the future and the state of your relationship with each other.

If you know for certain that your marriage is over, but you do not want to divorce – perhaps for religious reasons – then you can apply for a *judical separation.*

Before it can be granted, you have to be able to prove any of the five grounds that apply if you were petitioning for divorce (see page 51), although you don't have to prove the 'irretrievable breakdown' of your marriage, since a judicial separation does *not* put an end to your marriage in the way that divorce does, and does *not* leave you free to remarry. A judicial separation will not prevent your wife from divorcing you, though, on 'five years separation without consent' if she can't offer any other 'proof'.

If you both agree that divorce is the answer, and plan to go ahead with it right away, assuming you can agree on interim arrangements for the children, and maintenance, you don't need any formal agreement, but where money is concerned it's a good idea to ask the court to formalise your agreement in a consent order, which will benefit you both from an income tax point of view (see page 97).

If there is going to be a delay in the divorce proceedings, then you can apply for a formal separation order, which covers maintenance, custody of the children and access to them, and should include a clause releasing you and your wife from the 'marital duty to cohabit' – the obligation to live together which being married implies. That means you will not be able to divorce each other on the grounds of desertion, but the main advantage of a formal separation order is the money you'll save on tax.

If you and your wife haven't yet started divorce proceedings, and can't agree about how much maintenance you should pay her (or vice versa if she's working and you're minding the children, though it's almost always the other way round), then she can apply in the local magistrates' court for a maintenance order.

She will have to go to court, and fill in a form, stating her case. The magistrates will then issue a summons for you to appear in court to defend her claim for maintenance. The fact that you are summonsed, does *not* mean your wife will automatically be awarded maintenance.

You both appear at a court hearing held in private, in front of a panel of three lay magistrates or a stipendiary (full-time, paid) magistrate at which you'll both be questioned about your financial position.

Before they award any maintenance, the magistrate/s must be satisfied that you have failed to maintain your wife and children at a reasonable level if you are still living together, *or* that you have behaved in such a way that she can't reasonably be expected to go on living with you, *or* that you have deserted her.

If they are satisfied that any of these conditions apply, they will decide how much you should pay your wife and children.

In deciding the amount, the magistrate/s use the same guidelines these days as the divorce courts (see page 87) though magistrates tend to be less generous, and more influenced by your own and your wife's behaviour – perhaps because until very recently, a wife who had committed adultery was not entitled to *any* maintenance in the magistrates' courts!

If you and your wife have started divorce proceedings, and can't agree about the amount of maintenance you should pay while you're waiting for the final court hearing, then your wife can apply to the divorce court for 'maintenance pending suit' for herself and the children. Once she has made her application to the court, you will be given fourteen days in which to produce an 'affidavit of means' – a sworn statement giving details of your income, outgoings and so on (see page 85). Then, at a private hearing, the Registrar (in effect, a junior judge) will listen to both you and your wife, and make a decision. The amount of 'maintenance pending suit' is awarded 'as the court thinks reasonable', though in practice it will usually be less than you will have to pay under the final settlement. Registrars take the view that if it is too low, they can always compensate your wife by back-dating the final order, whereas if it's too high, they are realistic enough to know that there is little chance of your wife giving you a refund!

If your case drags on, both you and your wife can go back to court and ask for the amount to increased or decreased, but the order will stay in force until the divorce is finalised, and if the financial settlement isn't finalised at the same time, then the payments continue at the same level, but are called 'interim periodic payments' instead!

If you and your wife can agree about the interim arrangements for the children – where they should live and how often they should see the other parent – then there is no need to involve the courts at all. But of course, when most couples separate, there is usually some anger, and it is all too easy for it to focus on the children. If your wife has left you with the children and you feel she might come back and try to take them, you can apply for an interim custody order at the divorce court. (You can also apply in the magistrates' court, but many people feel that matters concerning the children are best dealt with by professionals.) It is worth considering, even if you don't think it's likely that your wife will try and take the children.

'I had a case recently where the wife had gone off with the husband's brother,' said a divorce court welfare officer, 'leaving him with the children. I was called in and suggested that he got an interim custody order. He said, "What for? She's said she won't take the children." And I had to say, "She says that now, but after living in a grotty bedsitter for a few weeks, she may well change her mind and want the children – and of course, the house." I don't want to sound cynical, but in my experience, that's what often happens. In fact, I was right – she did apply for the custody of the children, and the house, but in the end, although the judge was very reluctant to do it, he did leave the children with the father.'

If your wife has the children, and is making it impossible for you to see them, you should apply to the divorce court right away for an interim access order. It can take months for a divorce to come to court and for the children's future to be settled finally, and you can't afford to go without seeing them for that long. Even a few months in the life of a small child is an eternity, and a toddler may not even recognise you, which makes it extremely difficult to re-establish the kind of relationship with your children that you, and they, badly need.

But ideally before the difficulties over the children are allowed to become established, you should seek help from your local conciliation service, if there is one, because conciliation's main function is to help separating parents sort out their children's future *together*, without bitterness and anger.

As Dr Martin Richards of the Child Care and Development Group in Cambridge puts it, 'In the turmoil and confusion of separation, it is hardly surprising that the parents' own fears and desires may sometimes override a more reasoned approach to their children's needs. It is just such conflicts that conciliation is often able to sort out!'

3

Conciliation

In the last year or two, there has been a lot of talk about conciliation, and a number of conciliation services have been established in various parts of the country (see page 152 for list). Some are run by probation officers in their role as divorce court welfare officers, some by Marriage Guidance, and some independently, and they vary slightly in how they operate and what are willing to do. They all share the same basic aim, though, which Lisa Parkinson, founder and co-ordinator of the Bristol Courts Family Conciliation Service, sums up as 'assisting divorcing and separating couples to resolve disputes, and reach agreed decisions on specific issues arising from the breakdown of their marriage (or established relationship), especially in matters involving the children.'

Some conciliation services will also try to help resolve disputes over property and money, since they do affect the children, but most will only deal with the specific questions of custody, care and control, and access.

It's important to remember that a conciliator is a negotiator, *not* an arbitrator – in other words, his or her role is to help you and your wife come to an agreement that you both accept, not to listen to both sides of the story, and then reach a decision which is imposed on you.

Even where the conciliation service is linked to the divorce court, and even if the judge suggests that you and your wife go along to conciliation during the course of your divorce hearing, it is *completely independent* of the court. All the discussions you and your wife have with your conciliator are strictly confidential, and will not be disclosed to anyone, though of course any final decisions you both reach about the children's future will be passed on to the court.

Some parents who have been through conciliation feel that

confidentiality and independence from the court are essential.

'I wouldn't have felt able to be anything like as honest or as open,' said one father, 'if I'd felt that what I said might "be taken down and used in evidence against me" as it were, if the case did come to court.'

But other people feel that without some kind of legal back-up to enforce the agreements reached, it is really a waste of time.

'We went along to conciliation to sort out the children's future,' said one father who initially wanted to fight for care and control of his three children, 'and my wife made all the right noises, said I could see the children whenever I liked and that she would positively encourage them to see me if I agreed not to fight for them. I gave in, but she just isn't living up to her promises at all – in fact, she's making it as difficult for me as she can – and as she says she won't go back to conciliation, there's nothing they can do. They certainly can't make her abide by what was agreed.'

Conciliation shouldn't be confused with *re*conciliation – bringing couples back together again – although the Bristol conciliation service has found that one in six of the couples they see, do get back together as a result.

That's what happened to Tim and his wife Jane. When Tim first went to see a conciliator, Jane had left him after three years of marriage and was refusing to let him see their baby son. 'At first, Jane refused to go along to conciliation because she felt we should be able to sort out our problems ourselves, but whenever we tried to talk we just wound up arguing. It got worse and worse, and finally, as a last resort really, she agreed to go.

'We went separately at first, and I must say the first two sessions I had were a revelation to me. The conciliator helped me to see Jane's point of view which I simply hadn't been able to do before, and made me realise that so much that had gone wrong between us was due to a lack of any real communication. And because we couldn't communicate, we couldn't understand each other, so when the problems started, we just blamed each other, and that drove us further and further apart. As a result of conciliation, Jane and I were able to talk – really talk for the first time, and a few months later, we got back together again.'

Tim and his wife were lucky. They were referred to conciliation early on in their difficulties, before the layers of misunderstanding and bitterness had built up to such an extent that the marriage was beyond saving.

Even if you both know for sure that your marriage is beyond saving, but can't agree about the children's future, it is just as important to get help from a conciliation service as soon as you can, for precisely the same reasons.

As Lisa Parkinson says, conciliation should be 'the first resort, not a last-ditch attempt.' Once things start going wrong, and you and your wife start to take up entrenched positions over the children, making accusation and counter-accusation, it can be almost impossible to sort it all out. Getting help before you reach that point can prevent so much unhappiness. As one father wrote to the Bristol conciliators, 'The service made it easy for me to see my daughter without going to court, and it had smoothed the way if there is to be a divorce. The bitterness that was building up between us is now a thing of the past.'

Jacqueline Burgoyne and her colleague David Clark have found in their research into second marriages that, in nearly every case, disputes that arose at the time of separation had 'profound and long-term consequences both for the children and the adults concerned when they remarried.'

By the time Alan and his wife were recommended to try conciliation, he had been forced out of the family home by an exclusion order and hadn't been allowed to see his children for months. 'When those sort of things have happened, it is extremely hard to put aside the bitterness and sort it all out. Had we gone along, right at the start, conciliation might have been able to do something for us, but as it was, it was just too late.'

With most conciliation services, you can go along of your own accord, or on the recommendation of your solicitor, or the local Citizen's Advice Bureau. Most services do recognise the urgency, and will give you an appointment within a couple of days, if not the same day. You are free to go along *at any stage* in your divorce. In some divorce courts Registrars operate a system known as the pre-trial review (see page 80), or in-court conciliation, where they will invite you and your wife along to a meeting at which they, or a divorce court welfare officer will attempt to mediate between you, in the hope of sorting out disputes over the children without the need for a full court hearing. In other areas, once the hearing is underway, the judge may suggest that you try conciliation, and once the divorce is finalised, and you are having problems with access, conciliation may well be able to help you sort them out, whether the service helped you work the arrangements out in the first place or not.

If you go to a conciliation service before you have taken legal advice they may well encourage you to see a solicitor, one who is sympathetic to their work naturally, since it would be counter-productive to involve a solicitor who believes divorce should be all-out war. Although conciliators have a working knowledge of family law, they are not qualified to give legal advice, and besides, many feel it is important for you to have someone on your side, looking after your interests, as well as a neutral third party, helping you both reach agreement about the children's future.

Some conciliators will see the whole family – your new partners, and the children, since they are all concerned in the future arrangements – but others prefer to work with just husband and wife. It is essential that you both go along, since it is impossible to conciliate with one, although some conciliators will see you separately at first, if you prefer.

'The reason we don't usually see couples together at the start,' said Lisa Parkinson, 'is that after a marriage has broken down there is a lot of grief and pain, even it is hidden under anger. If we saw people together, they just wouldn't be able to let that come out because it would make them too vulnerable.'

She has also found in the four years the service has been running, that couples come to conciliation with mixed feelings. 'You often find there is a very fine balance between constructive feelings – wanting to find the best solution for the children – and destructive feelings – wanting to punish the other partner for what's happened. What we try and do is work on the common ground between them – wanting the best for the children – and try to prevent them giving way to the destructive feelings.'

You might think that conciliation can only work for couples who are at least on speaking terms, and so if communication between you and your wife has completely broken down, there's not point in going to a conciliation service because she won't agree to take part. But that may well not be the case.

Lisa Parkinson and her colleagues often find that the partner who they've been told simply won't want to know, responds immediately to their letter offering an appointment, and accepts it readily. 'Perhaps just to hint in the letter that their partner thinks they won't come is enough!'

She believes that many parents are aware that continuing deadlock isn't going to solve anything, and an offer of conciliation enables them to try and resolve it without losing face, and to separate the end of their marriage from their continuing responsibilities as parents. Any agreement you manage to reach with the help of conciliation has no legal status, but you can go to court and ask for a consent order which gives the arrangements you've agreed on the force of law. As a divorce court welfare officer put it, 'Consent orders are worth their weight in gold, because not only do they do away with the need for a contested court hearing, and the mud-slinging that inevitably involves, but it's my experience that people are much more likely to go along with a settlement they've been involved in reaching than they are with something that's imposed on them.'

Conciliation is still in its infancy, but detailed research done on the work in Bristol suggests that it is achieving remarkable results. In over eighty per cent of cases, parents were able to reach agreement about at least one major area of dispute, and in half the cases, they reached agreement on all issues.

Behind those statistics, there are hundreds of children – and adults – who will survive divorce far less damaged than they would otherwise have been so the saving in terms of long-lasting unhappiness makes conciliation an urgent priority. But it also represents a mammoth financial saving, too. Research suggests that the average cost of conciliation per person is about £46, whereas the legal aid costs for a contested custody hearing are nearer £450 a person.

Not surprisingly, with the civil legal aid bill expected to reach *£62.2 million* this year, the government has set up an inter-departmental committee to look at the possibility of a national conciliation service which is due to report in April 1983. But at the time of writing there are no plans to publish its findings, and anyway, it now seems likely that any decision will be postponed until another committee, set up to look at procedure in divorce cases, has finished its work in 1984. In the meantime, the Bristol conciliation service is yet again under threat of closure through lack of funds, with government departments all saying that of course it is a good thing, but they haven't got any money to finance it.

But, as Lisa Parkinson says, and all the evidence backs her up, it's not a question of whether we can afford to have conciliation services. We can't afford *not* to have them!

4

Telling the Children

Telling the children that you and your wife are going to separate is one of the most difficult and painful aspects of the whole process. Whatever justification you both feel you may have for leaving each other, there is no justification for leaving the children – which is how they will see it – and the resulting guilt is more than many parents can cope with. On top of that, you know that your children are going to need your love and reassurance more than ever before, and yet your own unhappiness and anxiety about the future make it more difficult for you to give it.

As a result, some parents do duck the issue. A survey carried out by *Woman* magazine in spring 1982, found that one parent in ten hadn't even told their children they were divorced, and one in four hadn't said anything to the children until after one parent had already moved out. In the course of his research, Mervyn Murch found that over a third of the parents interviewed hadn't talked to their children about the divorce at all, and of those who had, over half hadn't done so until after they had separated.

Some parents don't say anything for fear of upsetting the children – and themselves, some don't believe the separation is permanent, and so don't want to upset the children unnecessarily, while others feel there's no need to say anything because the children must know. But what may be obvious to you as an adult, may not be obvious to your children at all. To them, the fact that one of you has disappeared from the home with no explanation does *not* necessarily mean that you and your wife have decided that you can't go on living together any more, and they may well invent far more distressing explanations for themselves – you've gone because you don't love them any more, or they were so naughty that they drove you away.

Your decision to separate may well have come at the end of months of tension, rows and unhappiness, and though you may have prided yourself on never arguing in front of the children, they may well have realised that something is wrong. Many modern houses and flats have paper-thin walls, and they may have heard raised voices after they've gone to bed, or seen black faces at breakfast. And don't forget, children are much more sensitive to atmosphere than adults – even tiny babies' behaviour can be affected by tension in the home. If no-one tells them what's wrong, they will invent reasons for themselves, which are usually even more distressing than the truth.

In their book *I'm Leaving*, Bente and Gunnar Oberg report one example. An eight-year-old boy became aware that his parents had stopped joking and playing with him like they used to, and heard them talking in hushed, depressed voices night after night, when they thought he was asleep. He became convinced that they were criminals, plotting terrible deeds, and if they found out that he knew, they would kill him. When the parents finally decided to tell him they were going to separate, and started by saying they had some news for him that would make him very sad, the boy started screaming hysterically, 'No, I don't want to hear it, I don't want to know anything. You cannot kill me!' Eventually, they managed to tell the boy they had been trying to sort out their problems for some time, and hadn't wanted to say anything to him until they were certain that separation was the only answer.

'Slowly the boy emerged from his corner. "Then you're not robbers? You're not going to kill me?" It took a long time for all three of them to grasp how playing hide-and-seek with feelings can create even greater anxiety – anxiety about the unknown!'

If you can tell the children *together*, without arguing or shouting, so much the better. If not, then try to agree on what you'll say and tell them separately.

When should you tell the children?

Ideally, you should tell the children as soon as you decide to separate, and before one of you actually moves out. Of course, once the decision is made, you may well want to leave as soon as possible, but if you can, do give the children some warning that you're going. Simply telling them you're moving out that day gives them no time at all to adjust to the idea. You might think that staying around is just prolonging the agony for all of you, but in the long-term, it may be less distressing for the children to see how difficult and painful it is for you to leave them, rather than to think that you couldn't get away from them fast enough, or just couldn't care less.

That's the impression Judy got when her parents separated when she was eleven. 'My father was going to America on a business trip the next day, but there had been a lot of tension in the house for some time, so I asked him, "Are you coming back?" He said, "No. I'm going to live there."'

Don't try to hide your feelings from your children. Tell them how unhappy you are to be leaving them – it will be distressing for them, and for you, but much less hurtful than feeling it doesn't affect you at all.

If it just isn't possible to tell the children before one of you moves out, then tell them as soon as possible, and tell them the truth. Don't say, 'Mum's gone on holiday,' or, 'She's had to go away on business,' because the truth will come out, and it's much more distressing for the children to hear it from the neighbours, or other children at school. Besides, they will resent the fact that you lied to them, and it may shake their trust in you.

Caroline's father left home when she was seven, and her mother told her and her sister that the firm had sent him abroad on business very suddenly. 'A few weeks became a few months, and we didn't get the postcards we usually got, and so we started badgering her with questions – Why didn't he write? When was he coming home? In the end, she lost her temper, and told us the truth – that they were getting divorced, and he had been living in London all the time. It took me a long time to forgive either of them. When I finally asked my father why he'd walked out like that, without a word, he said he knew it was cowardly, but he just couldn't face us. It would have broken his heart, he said, to have seen our little faces when he said he was leaving. I understand but I still think what he did was wrong.'

What should you tell the children?

It may sound obvious, but do make sure that you explain what's going to happen in language you know the children will understand. If you tell your children that you and Mum are going to separate, you may get no reaction at all – not because they're not bothered, but because they don't know what 'separate' means. You do have to spell it out, even though it is very painful for you. 'We're separating' doesn't sound as bad as 'I'm not going to be living here with you all any more' but that is the reality.

Once you're sure the children have understood, then the most important thing to tell them, and to go on telling them, is that regardless of what has happened between you and their mother, you both still love them, will go on loving them, and there is no reason why they can't go on loving both of you. But if that is going to be a reality, then what you tell the children is crucial. How can they go on loving both of you if your wife is telling them it all went wrong because you're a womanising drunk, and you're telling them it wouldn't have happened if their mother wasn't a nagging shrew.

Although it is extremely difficult sometimes, do try not to be vindictive. If your wife has left you for another man, don't say to the children, 'Your mother obviously couldn't care less about you, or she'd never have gone off with that man!' or, 'I don't want you to think badly of your mother, so I won't go into detail about what she's done . . .' Instead, explain that although you did love each other once, your wife doesn't love you any more (or you don't love each other) and so you can't make her happy. That's why you can't go on living together, although you both still love them and will go on loving them, regardless. By making it clear that all the difficulties are between you and your wife, not between either of you and the children, it will at least stop them thinking that they are the cause of the problem.

At the same time, don't concentrate entirely on your own problems and emotions because what will concern the children most is how the divorce is going to affect them. They will want to know where they'll live, who'll look after them, whether they'll still go to the same school, whether Granny will still be their Granny – the kind of questions that wouldn't occur to you, but since their world is being turned upside down, they can no longer take anything for granted, and so all these things will be uppermost in their minds.

Do talk to them about their future, and if you're not sure whether they'll be living with you or your wife, then say so and don't make promises you may not be able to keep. Find out what their feelings and preferences are if you can, but don't ask them to make a straight choice. Having to choose between the two people you love most is too painful for any child, whose answer would probably be: 'I don't want to live with you *or* Mum – I want to live with both of you!'

If you are feeling very bitter and hurt about the separation, it is extremely tempting to try and win the children's sympathy and loyalty by telling them how badly your wife has behaved. But resist it if you possibly can. Just think how distressing it must be for the children, on top of everything else, to be told that their mother is no good, or couldn't care less about them.

If you're the one who's left, and you gather that your wife has been running you down to the children, don't retaliate by attacking her. Instead, repeat your reasons for leaving, and explain that their mother is only saying those things because she is hurt and unhappy, in the same way they say nasty things about their friends when they've had a quarrel.

As for how much you should tell the children, child psychiatrist Dr Robin Benians believes 'everything'. Children only understand what they're mature enough to understand, and everything else goes over their heads, but they will feel much more respected, and therefore loved, if they are told what's going on. Don't forget, children often know far more than parents think they do.'

When Keith's marriage broke down, after he became involved with another woman, he felt it was essential to be honest with the children. 'I told them that I wasn't leaving *them*, but that Liz had asked me to leave, quite rightly, because I was making her so unhappy by the way I was behaving. My son, who was then eight, asked me if I'd stopped loving Liz, and I said I hadn't, but like a lot of blokes, I was being stupid and greedy because I wanted more, and just couldn't stop myself.

'A few weeks ago, there was a play on television about a married man who was having an affair, and my son, who's now eleven, said, "Here, Dad, that bloke's just like you – stupid and greedy!"'

Be honest about what's happened, without being vindictive or making judgements. If the children have witnessed terrible scenes, then explain that they happened because being together was making you both so desperately unhappy.

Don't try and gloss over the problems, though. If you say that you've separated because you weren't getting on any more, the children may find it very hard to understand why you're staying apart. After all, they fall out with their friends all the time, and say they never want to speak to them again ever, but next day, they make up.

If you make the problems sound too trivial, or keep stressing what a wonderful person your wife is, and how much you both still care about each other, the children will be very confused about why you had to separate in the first place.

Make it clear that you understand they will be upset by what's happened and that you are willing to answer any questions they may have. If you try and make light of what has happened, then the children may be afraid to express their unhappiness, or make it clear by your attitude that you really don't want to talk about it, then they will have to bottle it all up inside, which is even more distressing.

At the same time, respect their privacy, and don't pry. If they seem not to want to talk about it, then don't press them. If they do ask questions, answer them honestly, but don't give more information than they've asked for. If they ask, 'Where's Mum living now?', tell them the address or the location, but don't use it as the pretext for a diatribe about 'the man who's wrecked our lives'!

You may find, especially if the children are very young, that they don't take it in all at once. In the course of her research, Sheila Burns came across a family of four, now grown up, whose parents separated when they were twelve, ten, eight and five. 'The oldest three told me they were *all* called into their parents' bedroom one Sunday morning, and given the bad news, but the youngest one says she wasn't told. She has no recollection of that Sunday morning at all.'

How the children may react

Children's initial reaction to the news that their parents are going to separate can be very varied, so you should be prepared for almost anything.

If things have been very bad between you and your wife for some time, then their initial reaction may be relief that the tension and uncertainty are going to be resolved, though that may well change once they realise that the price for ending the tension is losing one of you from their daily lives. One famous study done in California by Judith Wallerstein and Joan Berlin

Kelly, and described in their book *Surviving the Breakup*, followed divorcing families over a five-year period, and found no children who were glad their parents had divorced, and only a few were expressed relief, even though a number of the marriages had involved dreadful rows, and even violence.

Your children might be visibly upset – crying, clinging, begging you not to go – or they might become violently angry with both, or either of you.

When Steve and his wife Mary told their five-year-old son they were separating, he reacted by flying at Steve and punching him in the stomach, and when Mary tried to grab hold of him, he knocked her arms aside and ran from the room. 'He was shouting that he hated us, and that we weren't his Mummy and Daddy any more, and for the rest of the day, he wouldn't speak to either of us. After that, his behaviour alternated between fits of rage and wanting Mary to "baby" him, feeding him with a spoon, cradling him in her arms. It was very confusing.'

It is quite a common reaction for children to 'regress' – to start behaving like babies, forgetting their toilet training, wanting to be fed, and held all the time. 'It's the sort of behaviour that's often called "attention seeking",' said Dr Benians, 'but children do it because they *need* the attention of the remaining parent. The best way of coping with it is to go along with it, because it meets some of your needs too. The physical closeness can be very comforting.'

Some children show no reaction at all. It's tempting to breathe a huge sigh of relief and think that they've just accepted it because, of course, it makes life so much easier for you, but in many ways it's the most worrying reaction of all, and chances are there will be problems – disruptive behaviour, depression, inability to concentrate – later on. While you shouldn't watch your children like a hawk for the slightest sign of disturbance, do be aware that problems can crop up long after you'd thought everything was sorted out.

If you are worried about your children, then don't be afraid of seeking help. If the school is sympathetic, that may be a good place to start, or your family doctor may be able to refer you to a local child guidance clinic. Don't think that your children will be labelled as 'unstable' or 'problem children' as a result. In the same way that adults can benefit from counselling in getting over a major crisis, like divorce, so can children.

In the long-term, children's reactions to divorce vary according to a number of factors, including their age. Even though Wallerstein and Kelly's study was done in California, and there are differences between there and here, it is a very useful guide to the kind of reactions to expect.

They found that children under six, roughly, were confused and frightened, terrified that since one parent had left them, the other might too, and they often blamed themselves for what had happened. They also cling on to the hope that their parents will get back together again. Children between six and nine felt sad and rejected, and though they often felt very angry with their parents – for leaving, or for driving the other parent away – they were often afraid to express it, and took it out on brothers or sisters, or friends instead. They, too, longed for their parents to get back together again.

Slightly older children were more able to express their anger with their parents, and though they didn't feel to blame for what had happened, they felt ashamed, and the fact that lots of other children's parents are divorced didn't make any difference. They often felt torn between their parents, and lonely and rejected.

Adolescents were often the most openly upset by their parents' separation, and expressed very forcibly their anger, sadness and shame. In 1982, Judith Wallerstein carried out a ten-year follow-up study on the same group of children, now in their teens and early twenties. She hasn't yet published her final conclusions, but her preliminary report suggests that most the young people still see their parents' divorce as a continuing, major influence in their lives, and many still feel a deep sadness and a yearning for the family life they feel they missed.

From several recent studies, done here and in the United States, it's clear that what matters most to children after divorce, and what affects their mental and emotional well-being is the quality of their relationships with *both* their parents, and not the fact that the parents don't get on, or even still fight. And those children who get over divorce and its consequences most quickly, and with least damage, are those who still have good relationships with both parents.

Although what you tell your children is very important, it's what you *do* that matters most. If you tell them that, although you won't be living with them any more, you st and you will see each other often, what will convinc you mean it is seeing you often.

Divorce can be a devastating experience for you but it needn't be – as long as you and your wife underst needs and are prepared to put their interests first.

School

It is a good idea to let your children's teachers know what is happening at home as soon as you decide to separate, rather than waiting until the divorce goes through. You might be reluctant to say anything for fear that the children might be labelled as coming from 'a broken home', or you may simply find it embarrassing to discuss your personal problems with an authority figure. But remember that there will be a number of children at the school with divorced parents, and that some of the teachers will be divorced themselves.

If your children's teachers know there are problems at home, then they will be able to make allowances if there are behaviour difficulties or if the standard of their school work suddenly declines. For many children, school can provide a retreat from the turmoil at home during the divorce, but if they're in trouble there, too, because no-one knows what's behind it, it can be doubly distressing.

Not all children show signs of distress at school, but it's worth talking to their teachers, just in case.

5

Solicitors

'My solicitor had a print on his office wall. It showed a cow being tugged by two litigants, one was pulling its head, and one was pulling its tail, and there was a figure in a wig, sitting underneath the cow, milking it. And that sums up my feelings perfectly – I was milked!'

That's a sentiment you often hear expressed by divorced men, and although a research project showed that the majority of people were satisfied with the way solicitors had handled their divorce, there is a considerable minority who are very dissatisfied indeed. They feel that the solicitors had a financial interest in dragging out their case, or that they didn't argue it as forcefully as they should have done, or that they gave in to the other side on everything, or even that they were responsible for turning what had been a reasonably civilised separation into all-out war.

That's certainly how Bob feels about his ex-wife's solicitor. 'We had agreed to divorce on the basis of two years separation with consent, and as this was before 1977, when it was still possible to get legal aid for an undefended divorce, we agreed that she would petition, since she would be eligible for legal aid and I wouldn't.

'Next thing I knew, I received a letter from her solicitor saying that she was divorcing me on the grounds of my 'unreasonable behaviour' and enclosing a sworn statement listing all my 'crimes' over the fifteen years of our marriage, most of them totally false, and the few that had some basis in truth were wildly distorted or exaggerated. I was outraged.

'Later, I gathered from a mutual friend that what had happened was the solicitor had asked whether she really wanted to wait the two years, and when she'd said, No, not if she didn't have to, he'd asked whether I had ever committed adultery, and because she said I hadn't, he'd said, "Well, what about unreasonable behaviour? Has he ever behaved unreasonably?" My wife did tell this friend that she hadn't wanted to include a lot of things in the petition, but the solicitor had insisted, saying that it was the only way to get the petition through the court. Of course, that put paid to any hope of keeping things reasonably amicable.'

David's divorce nearly turned into war when his solicitor wrote to his wife, going back on the agreement they had reached at the start, that she should have their flat, outright. 'She rang a friend of ours, absolutely furious, to tell her what I'd done. The friend suggested she talked to me but she said she was so angry she would never speak to me again. The friend had no qualms about "interfering" fortunately, and told me what was happening. I was appalled – I'd no idea my solicitor had written that letter. All he's said to me was that he was going to finalise the property settlement. When I tackled him about it, he said he was acting in my best interest because I was being too generous. I changed solicitors at once, rang my wife and explained, and luckily we were able to repair the damage that had been done.'

Playwright Terence Frisby, who claims the legal profession created the years of struggle over money, custody and access in his case, feels so passionately about lawyers, that his advice to anyone thinking of consulting them about divorce is 'Don't – and if you already have, then sack 'em! If I'd done that right at the start of my divorce, then my whole life since then would have been very different.

'Ask yourself what you need a solicitor for? To tell you about legal procedure? The court officials can tell you that. To sort out money and property? An accountant can give you better advice, and if you and your wife can't agree, present the judge all the figures and let him decide. To sort out the children's future? What do solicitors know about the welfare of children? Nothing! My experience tells me loud and clear that you're better off without them!'

He represented himself in a number of High Court hearings, as did David, who was also involved in custody battles over his only child, though, with the benefit of hindsight, he has mixed feelings about it. 'There are advantages, certainly. You can write as many letters as you like to the other side's solicitors and it doesn't cost you a penny, and because you don't know all the legal technicalities and jargon, your letters flummox them!

'When I represented myself in court, I had every single detail of the case at my fingertips, whereas my wife's barrister had only arrived ten minutes before the hearing, and it soon became clear that he wasn't on top of it at all.

'But on the other hand, my lack of legal experience did let me down. At one point the judge said something about not intending to talk to my daughter about her feelings on the subject "unless either parent invites me to." I didn't understand that he was formally offering to see her if I asked him to, so I let it pass. He awarded custody to my wife, although my daughter had been living with me and wanted to go on doing so, and in the judgement he said that he had been prepared to see the child, but neither parent had invited him to. A barrister would have understood what the judge was saying, and would have taken up the offer. Had the judge talked to my daughter, then the outcome might have been different.'

But most people whose marriages have run into serious difficulties do want professional help. Even if you haven't decided finally that the marriage is over or that divorce is the only answer, you may want to know what your legal position would be, and consult a solicitor. There is evidence to suggest that people with marriage problems consult solicitors for advice and help with *non*-legal aspects of those problems, probably because they feel that seeing a solicitor doesn't carry the same social stigma as consulting other professionals like probation officers or social workers.

'We have come across a growing number of cases,' said Gwynn Davies of the Department of Social Administration at Bristol University, 'where couples have been reconciled *after* they have petitioned for divorce, which could mean that people are using the legal system to bring their marriage problems out into the open, and to help sort them out.'

If you haven't made up your mind that you want a divorce, you may be lucky and consult a solicitor who understands that fact, and will be willing to talk through the problems with you. In fact, some solicitors do say that where divorce is concerned, three-quarters of their time is spent counselling rather than giving strictly legal advice.

Other solicitors will realise that you are undecided, but don't have the time or the expertise to counsel you themselves, and so will refer you to Marriage Guidance, or a conciliation service if there is one in your area, or any other form of counselling that is available (solicitors are required by law to discuss the possibility of reconciliation with you, but that can vary from a long discussion about your problems in the marriage to 'And there's no possibility of reconciliation, is there?'). Tim believes that his solicitor and the conciliation service between them, saved his marriage.

'When I went to see the solicitor first off, I was convinced my marriage was over, and I was determined to get "my rights". But she kept saying, "Let's not rush into anything. Have you really thought about what it will mean? Have you considered how your wife must feel?" and persuaded me to try conciliation before I did anything else. After a couple of sessions with them, on our own first, then together, we've been able to communicate with each other for the first time, really, and sort it all out. If it hadn't been for my solicitor, though, I'd have been a divorced – and very unhappy – man by now.'

Bill wasn't so lucky. He was devastated to discover his wife was having an affair and went along to a solicitor for some advice. 'I really just wanted someone to talk to about it all, but by the time I left his office, he'd already drawn up a petition, on the grounds of my wife's adultery, and the whole machinery had been set in motion. I could have stopped it I suppose, but I wasn't thinking straight. I don't think my wife had finally decided what she wanted to do, either, but when she got the letter from my solicitor, it made the decision for her. Had I seen a different solicitor, I think my marriage might well have been saved.'

One explanation is that solicitors are trained in the law, and so the only solution to marriage problems with which many of them are familiar – and comfortable – is a legal one, divorce.

Solicitors aren't trained as counsellors or conciliators, it's true, but it's not unreasonable to expect people who choose to work in the painful, emotional area of divorce to show some sensitivity.

Peter went to consult a solicitor late one afternoon in a desperate state because he had just discovered that his ex-wife had applied for permission to emigrate with their two young children, which would mean, essentially, that he would never see them again.

'I was absolutely distraught, and at one stage in the conversation this chap said, "Would you excuse me for a moment – I must just go and ring my children to say 'goodnight'."'

Another father was involved in a bitter custody battle in the High Court when his wife's barrister said, jokingly, 'I cannot understand why this father is so keen to hold on to his children. I would be quite pleased if someone were to take mine!'

Many people believe it is the way solicitors are trained and the way the legal system operates which actually encourages divorcing couples to fight.

Ironically divorces are 'civil' cases, and all civil cases, according to a leading QC, are 'clearly defined war games, played according to well-settled rules, with a "winner" and a "loser", and the court acting as referee.'

Ours is an 'adversarial' system – not for nothing are divorce cases listed as 'Smith *versus* Smith' – and so solicitors and barristers are trained to do battle on their clients' behalf, fighting as dirty as the law permits, in order to get the best possible 'deal' for their clients.

'There are still a lot of solicitors who view divorce as merely another form of litigation,' said a solicitor with a busy divorce practice in London, 'where the way to do the best for their client is *not* to think about the state he or she will be in at the end, or the fact that, if there are children, the people involved will have to go on having some kind of relationship with each other once the legal battle is over, but to screw as big a share of the matrimonial home as possible out of the other side, or to get away with paying as little maintenance as you can. That kind of solicitor may do an ace job legally, but he is not doing his client any good at all!

'I personally don't see it as my job to stir up trouble, and I always hope to find a solicitor on the other side who wants to sort it all out without getting into court battles, and who sends amicable letters instead of aggressive, "sabre-rattling" ones. It doesn't happen often, sadly, but when it does it is so rewarding all round. Clients say: "It was still traumatic and painful and awful, but, compared to friends who've been divorced, at least I'm still comparatively sane!"'

So, finding the *right* solicitor is absolutely vital, but how do you go about it?

First of all, you need a solicitor with a lot of experience in divorce cases. The chap who handled the conveyancing on your house, no matter how efficient he was, probably isn't right, nor is the small firm in the High Street who do a 'bit of everything' because they are not going to be practised at dealing with all the emotional, social and financial complexities, let alone the legal ones. Nor will they be up to date with all the changes – not so much in the law itself, but in the way the courts are interpreting the law, which will affect the outcome of your divorce.

Solicitors aren't allowed to advertise so it's not easy to find out which firms specialise in divorce, but your local Citizen's Advice Bureau can help. They keep a list of all local solicitors, indicating the area of law in which they specialise, so you can see who specialises in divorce. Be a bit cautious though – at one Citizen's Advice Bureau a local solicitor, working on his own, had ticked *eleven* subjects as his specialities!

Officially, Citizen's Advice Bureaux are not allowed to recommend individual solicitors, but some will give you a list of three or four names, and though they won't actually *say* they recommend them, you can take it as read that they are known to be good.

Same with local law centres – they can't handle your divorce for you, though they will talk over any problems you want to discuss, and can put you in touch with solicitors they know from experience to be sympathetic and easy to talk to.

Your local branch of Families Need Fathers, the pressure group for equal parental rights, will also be a good source of advice. Most of their members are divorced men who will be able to recommend, from first hand experience, solicitors they've found to be good, and just as important, to steer you away from those who are bad.

Of course 'good' and 'bad' are pretty subjective terms, and it depends on what you expect from your solicitor. If you want him to be on your side, and to stand up for your rights – and many people do – then you won't think he's good if he tries to persuade you to compromise. As one father put it, 'I suppose I wanted him to get the best deal possible as far as I was concerned. I didn't want him standing up for the opposition. She's quite capable of that herself!'

On the other hand, if you hope to keep the divorce as civilised and as amicable as possible, then a solicitor who wants to fight over every penny, and writes hostile agressive letters to the other side, will be disastrous from your point of view.

'My solicitor kept saying things like "We can get her on this", even though I kept saying I didn't want my wife "got" on anything. Our marriage had broken down – as much my fault as hers – and I just wanted help on the legal steps necessary to end it. Finally I left him and went to another solicitor who understood what I was saying!'

According to a very experienced divorce solicitor, what you need is 'someone who thinks like you, who sees life in the same way that you do, with the same attitudes and experience of life that you have.'

Once you have found your solicitor, the most important thing to remember is that you are the client, that you are employing him or her, whether you are paying the bill yourself, or whether you are on legal aid, and therefore, what you say, ultimately, goes.

Some solicitors would argue that since that is the case, it is patently unfair to blame them for the bitterness and fighting that goes on in divorce because they are only obeying orders, and don't make any decisions themselves.

That is disingenuous, to say the least. You go to a solicitor because you don't know what to do and you need advice at a time when you are feeling very vulnerable emotionally, and in no fit state to make cool, calm rational judgements, so you are likely to go along with whatever he suggests. If his or her approach is aggressive and inflammatory, you will probably assume that's the way divorce is handled since you've had no previous experience of it and therefore wouldn't know there is another way.

The same is true of the legal advice you are given. You will probably accept it at face value because solicitors know the law and that's why you've gone along to see him or her.

If you are told that you stand no chance of getting joint custody of your children and therefore it's pointless even to try, you'll probably decide that it's not worth applying. If your solicitor doesn't even tell you there *is* such a thing as joint custody, the decision is made for you!

When one solicitor was asked why he didn't tell one father about the existence of joint custody, he replied, 'He didn't ask.'

It seems that you need to know the law before you seek legal advice!

If you know what you want, and what is possible, then you are free to reject your solicitor's advice, and insist that he/she does as you ask. But bear in mind that if he/she feels that you're asking for the impossible, then he/she is hardly likely to argue very powerfully in your cause.

'My own solicitor told me there was something "unhealthy" in my wanting to bring up my eight-year-old son myself,' said one father who wanted to apply for care and control, 'so you can imagine how hard he was going to try!'

If you're not happy with your solicitor's tactics then don't allow yourself to be persuaded to go along with them for the sake of expediency. After all, you're the one who has to live with the long-term consequences of mud-slinging affidavits or bitter court battles! Do remember you are free to change your solicitor at any time if you're not happy with the way he is conducting your case. If you are paying the legal fees yourself, your solicitor won't release your papers until you have paid his/her bill. Incidentally, if you feel you have been charged too much, you can ask the Law Society to 'tax' the bill for you, which means they will go through all the papers and decide what a reasonable charge for the amount of work done would be. If you're on legal aid, then you must contact the Law Society and tell them you are planning to change – to another solicitor on the legal aid scheme, obviously – and they will then transfer your legal aid certificate, and all your papers to the new solicitor. You won't be able to proceed until that has been done, so inevitably it will delay everything.

It's been said that changing solicitors is rather like changing deckchairs on the *Titanic*, because it is the whole system that is at fault, encouraging confrontation, not conciliation.

'It seems to me,' said Terence Frisby, 'that the present system is not just wrong, it's the complete opposite of what is needed. When a couple with children are breaking up, they are trying to divide the indivisible, and what they need is compassion, calmness – because they are both on a knife-edge, emotionally – and a caring but objective conciliatory approach. What do they get under the present set-up? Solicitors! And what are solicitors trained to do? Fight! What we need is a system of divorce that does away with lawyers altogether.'

For some years, there has been talk of special family courts, staffed by people trained not only in the law, but in the social sciences, where the approach would be *inquisitorial* – getting everyone involved round a table to try and find the best solution possible – rather than the adversarial system we have at present. The idea has had a lot of support, but in the present financial climate, the chances of it being implemented are as remote as ever.

For the time being, it's a question of making the best of the system we have, and trying to temper its worst excesses.

Mervyn Murch, from the Department of Social Administration at Bristol University, who has been examining the impact of divorce on families over the last ten years, believes that the involvement of solicitors *and* conciliators can solve at least some of the problems.

'When you are going through a divorce, feeling very vulnerable and threatened, you do need to feel that there is someone on your side, looking out for your interests. Many solicitors at the moment, do meet that need, but what they can't do, I feel, is also act as an impartial go-between, helping the couple work out their children's future.

'It seems to me that divorce is about transition from an old marriage into a new status, and you need people to guide you through it. It's like crossing a rickety old bridge, and needing two ropes to hang on to – one, the lawyer who's looking after your interests, and two, this impartial person, the conciliator, who'll address him or herself to the problems of the whole family.'

Finally, a word about barristers. If your divorce is contested, or there is to be a full court hearing about the children, property or money, your solicitor will suggest that you have a barrister to represent you. If the case goes to the High Court or the Court of Appeal, you will *have* to have a barrister – or represent yourself – since solicitors aren't allowed to appear in the higher courts. You are not allowed to approach a barrister direct – barristers can only 'take instructions' from solicitors – so your solicitor will decide who to employ. If you have heard that a particular barrister is especially good in cases like yours, you can ask your solicitor to approach him/her, but some busy, successful barristers tend to take instructions only from certain firms of solicitors, so you may have to go through one of those firms.

Even if you manage to get the barrister of your choice, there is no guarantee that he/she will be able to appear on the day of your hearing. If the previous case in which he/she is appearing goes on longer than expected, you will have to accept a substitute, which isn't ideal since he/she won't have much time to get to grips with the details of your case.

6

Divorce: The Law and the Legal Process

Before the divorce laws in England and Wales were reformed in 1969 (for Scotland and Northern Ireland, see page 149), the only way you could get a divorce was to prove your wife guilty of a 'matrimonial offence' – cruelty, mental or physical, adultery or desertion – and only the innocent party was entitled to start proceedings. What it meant was that there was no way out of a marriage that simply wasn't working any more if neither of you had committed a 'matrimonial offence', unless one of you was prepared to fake the evidence – hiring a call-girl to be photographed in bed with you by a private detective was a popular method. But since the 'guilty party' was likely to be penalised in the decisions about the children's future and the division of property and money, some people were unwilling to take that course.

As a result, thousands of people were trapped in dead marriages, living apart for years, often in another stable relationship from which they had children, but unable to cut the legal ties that still bound them to their former partner, and unable to marry again. The aim of the Divorce Reform Act 1969, was, according to the Law Commission, to give dead marriages 'a decent burial' and to ensure 'the maximum fairness and the minimum bitterness, distress and humiliation.' It accepted the reality that no-one is totally to blame for the failure of a marriage, and abolished the idea of the 'matrimonial offence', and of 'innocent' and 'guilty' parties. From 1 January 1971, when the new law came into force, there has been only one ground for divorce – the irretrievable breakdown of the marriage.

Before you can petition for divorce in England and Wales (for Scotland and Northern Ireland, see page 149), you must be 'domiciled' here, which means you must live here permanently, or if you have been living abroad (and that includes Scotland, Northern Ireland, the Isle of Man, and the Channel Islands) you *intend* to live here permanently. If you have been 'domiciled' elsewhere, then you must live here for at least a year before you can petition.

At the time of writing, you must have been married for at least three years before you could petition for divorce, unless you can prove 'exceptional depravity' on the part of your wife, or that you would suffer 'exceptional hardship' if you had to stay married for three years. But in the autumn of 1982, the government announced plans to change the law, so that you can petition after *one* year of marriage. The thinking is that if you are forced to wait three years, there is a greater risk of your having children, which is best avoided if the marriage is already doomed.

If you qualify both in terms of 'domicile' and length of marriage, then to get a divorce, you must be able to prove that your marriage has broken down irretrievably, and to do that, you must be able to offer one of the following five 'proofs'.

1 Adultery

You must be able to prove, not just that your wife has committed adultery, but that you find it intolerable to go on living with her as a result.

To prove adultery, you could hire a private detective to collect the evidence for you, but that will be expensive, and is hardly likely to keep the divorce proceedings reasonably civilised. Circumstantial evidence is usually enough – letters from your wife's lover to her, witnesses who've seen them holding hands or kissing, or have seen them together when your wife claimed she was somewhere else. But these days, since 'behaviour' is very unlikely to affect the court's decisions about the children's future, money and property, your wife will probably be willing to make a statement, admitting where and when and with whom she committed adultery. The courts don't allow the 'co-respondant' – your wife's lover – to hide behind the anonymity of 'Mr X' and will name him in court.

As for proving that you find it intolerable to go on living with your wife as a result of her adultery, it is usually enough for you simply to make a statement to that effect.

2 Unreasonable behaviour

This is the vaguest of all the 'proofs', and its vagueness means that it is used to cover anything other proofs can't reach! It includes the old grounds of physical and mental cruelty, addiction to drugs, drink or gambling, homosexuality, unreasonable sexual behaviour (like excessive sexual demands, refusal to have sex at all, sodomy, bestiality and so on), and refusing to have children. It can also include dirty habits – one woman was granted a divorce recently because her husband refused to bath or change his socks regularly – persistent nagging, unreasonably restricting rules – one man was granted a divorce because his wife wouldn't allow him to drink, smoke or watch television on Sundays! Although the law does say the behaviour complained of must be 'grave and weighty', almost anything can be used.

Proof of unreasonable behaviour varies, according to the circumstances. If your wife is petitioning on the grounds of your violence, then the court would require a doctor's certificate, stating the nature of her injuries, the date and time they were treated and what treatment was necessary. If you are petitioning because your wife's persistent sarcasm is affecting your health to such an extent that you've had to see the doctor, then get him or her to write a letter, confirming your visits, and stating what he believes to be the cause of your symptoms. Other people – friends, colleagues, relatives – may also be able to give evidence of the effect on you: weight loss, inability to concentrate, tearfullness and so on.

3 Desertion

In order to prove that your wife has deserted you, you must be able to show, *first*, that she left you over two years ago, *second*, that she left with the intention of deserting you (if she is in prison or in a mental hospital, then she hasn't deserted you), *third*, that you didn't want her to go, *fourth*, that you didn't give her reasonable cause for leaving you.

If you are offered a job that involves a move, and your wife refuses to go, then you *could* petition for divorce on the grounds of her desertion. But in the last few years, since many women have careers of their own, the courts no longer automatically assume that a woman should follow her husband, so each case is determined on its merits.

Desertion usually means that your wife has left home and is living somewhere else, but not always. In one case, the wife moved into the spare bedroom, which she kept locked, refused to do any housework for the husband and communicated with him only through notes. The judge decided that she had deserted her husband. In a similar case, though, where the wife had no contact with her husband, other than cooking him an occasional meal, the judge decided it was still one household, not two, and therefore the wife had not deserted her husband.

4 Two years separation with consent

This proof was very controversial when it was introduced in the 1969 Divorce Reform Act, because it allowed a couple to divorce by mutual consent, without having to prove that anyone was to blame. All they had to do was live apart for two years.

The two years begins from the time you decide the marriage is over. If you separate to try and sort things out, but decide after a couple of months that the marriage is over, then that's when the two years start, not on the date you actually separated.

It may be that, although you have decided that the marriage is over, it just isn't possible for one or other of you to move out of the home. You can both stay and still get a divorce on these grounds *provided* you set up completely separate households within the home – separate bedrooms and living rooms, and if you share the kitchen, you mustn't cook for each other, or eat together, otherwise the courts could say that you are still living in one household, not two.

5 Five years separation without consent

If you and your wife have been living apart for five years, and she won't agree to a divorce, then you can go ahead and divorce her anyway *unless* she can prove that she will suffer 'grave financial or other hardship' as a result. In practice the hardship has to be very grave indeed before the courts will refuse to grant the divorce. If, for instance, your wife will lose a generous widow's pension that she would have received on your death, and you can't afford to replace it (see page 89), the courts could refuse to grant the divorce.

The 'kiss and make-up' clause

With each of the five 'proofs' the law gives you a chance to live together again to try and sort out your differences, without it affecting your right to petition for divorce if the attempt at reconciliation fails.

In all cases, you are allowed a *total* of six months. Suppose you discover on Christmas Eve that your wife is having an affair. You decide that you won't divorce her, and carry on living together. By mid-January, though, you find you can't forgive and forget and so you move out. At the end of April, you think you have been too hasty, and so move back in again. But by the beginning of July, you realise it will never be the same again, and so decide that divorce is the answer. Although it is over six months since you discovered her unfaithfullness, you have only lived with your wife for less than three months in that time, so you can divorce her on the grounds of her adultery. Had you lived together for more than six months, the courts would consider that you had forgiven your wife, and therefore you wouldn't be able to divorce her on the grounds of that particular act of adultery. If she is unfaithful again, you could petition for divorce on the new evidence.

If you are petitioning on the grounds of two years separation with consent, and your attempt at reconciliation lasts for four months, then you will have to wait two years and four months from the date you originally separated.

The other way of ending your marriage legally is to seek an annulment, which states that your marriage was never legally valid, or it was defective from the start.

The grounds include:

being under sixteen at the time of the marriage
being married already
being too closely related
being of the same sex
being unable or unwilling to have sex
being mentally ill at the time of the marriage
being pregnant by another man and not admitting it
having a communicable form of venereal disease, and not admitting it.

It is comparatively rare – only about 1,000 petitions a year compared to 170,000 divorce petitions – but the courts can make the same sort of orders concerning children, property and money as they can in divorce cases.

When the Divorce Reform Act was introduced in 1969, it was condemned by some groups as a 'Casanova's Charter'. They forecast that the five years separation without consent provision would result in thousands of blameless middle-aged wives being cast aside in favour of a younger model. But it hasn't worked out that way.

In 1980, of the 12,589 divorces sought on those grounds, 5,884 were sought by men, and 6,705 by women.

Overall, of the 177,415 petitions filed, 49,921 were filed by men, and 127,494 were filed by women.

There is no simple explanation for the imbalance in the numbers of men and women petitioning for divorce. Some women's groups would argue it's because women are realising that marriage is a rotten deal. That may be true for some women, but the fact that the majority marry again, and quite quickly after divorce, suggests it's by no means true for all.

In some cases, where a couple agree on divorce and the wife isn't working, it makes sense for her to petition because she will get help with her legal costs, while her husband probably wouldn't. And there are still some men, usually older men, who still prefer to 'do the decent thing' and let their wives divorce them, regardless of who actually wants the divorce.

One of the main hopes for the Divorce Reform Act was that it would reduce the bitterness and fighting surrounding divorce, and the most important element in achieving that hope was the two years separation with consent provision. Although under the new law, the only ground for divorce was to be 'irretrievable breakdown', three of the 'proofs' – adultery, unreasonable behaviour, and desertion – involve one partner proving the other if not 'guilty', then at least responsible for the breakdown of the marriage. Two years separation with consent did away with the need to allocate blame, and therefore would enable a couple to divorce with as little bitterness and hostility as possible.

But it hasn't worked out like that. In 1980, only 40,000 couples (approximately) were divorced on that 'proof', while 45,000 divorced on adultery, and the largest group, almost 50,000, divorced using the 'proof' of unreasonable behaviour.

It isn't difficult to see why this 'proof' has become so popular. People who have decided that they want a divorce, often don't want to wait two years, and so, often at their solicitors' suggestion, they consider other 'proofs' that don't involve waiting – adultery and unreasonable behaviour. The former is a very specific activity, which has to be proved. The latter can – and often does – cover a multitude of minor sins, the sort of trivial things that are part and parcel of most marriages – happy and unhappy.

As one solicitor, happily married to another solicitor put it, 'We often say we could both draw up a ten-page affidavit (sworn statement) about the other's unreasonable behaviour *before breakfast*! Everything in it would be true, but exaggerated, distorted, taken out of context.

'In the hands of a good draughtsman – and please note I don't say "good solicitor"! – a behaviour affidavit can be devastating, and the person who receives this list of their "crimes" over the years feels totally outraged and betrayed. In fact, I'd say that if the marriage hadn't broken down irretrievably before, then once a behaviour affidavit has been sent, and read, it has! If I had the chance, I would do away with unreasonable behaviour as a "proof" tomorrow!'

A divorce court welfare officer working in the Home Counties, agrees. '"Unreasonable behaviour" is the biggest fiddle going in the divorce courts. The affidavits I see – Grimm's Fairy Tales, I call them – are full of half-truths. The woman who says, "My husband pushed the dinner down the table and swore at me," fails to mention that the dinner was two burnt sausages, left to go cold! I really do believe that an awful lot of the complaints people are encouraged to make in these affidavits are, frankly, absurd!'

If you receive an affidavit in which you are accused of things you simply didn't do, you will certainly be angry, but what can you actually do about it?

When David found himself in that position, he decided to fight it on a matter of principle. 'I felt the quality of the evidence offered in my wife's affidavit was appalling – it would have been laughed out of court in a criminal hearing – so I wrote back to her solicitors, requiring them to "put to proof" – in other words, to prove – the majority of allegations she was making.

Eventually, I received an amended affidavit from them, much, much shorter than the first!'

According to Yvonne Moffat, of the Campaign for Justice in Divorce, it is accepted officially, that over ninety per cent of affidavits in divorce cases are perjured – in other words, the person making the sworn statement is knowingly telling lies – and yet it is very rare for anyone to be prosecuted for perjury as a result.

How to get a divorce

This section assumes that you are the 'petitioner' – the one seeking the divorce. If you are the 'respondant' – the one being divorced – then for 'your wife', read 'you'.

The first stage is for your solicitor to draw up the petition (see page 64 for *Do it yourself divorce*), which states your own and your wife's full names, your occupations, when and where you were married, where you last lived together, and where you are living now, the names and ages of your children, which of you is to have custody, care and control, what arrangements you propose about the house, and maintenance, and why you believe your marriage has irretrievably broken down.

It will involve your solicitor asking you a lot of personal questions about your marriage, which you may find embarrassing, but remember his interest is strictly professional and that he has probably heard it all before dozens of time so won't be shocked. It is essential that you are completely honest with your solicitor, because what you tell him or her will form the basis of your petition. If you are planning to divorce your wife on the grounds of her desertion, and you fail to tell your solicitor that she left because you insisted on keeping ferrets in the bedroom, it will create appalling complications later on.

He/she will ask you about the arrangements you are proposing for the children's future – where they'll live, which schools they'll go to, how they will be supported, what arrangements you suggest for access to the children – and draw up a statement to that effect which you will then sign.

Your solicitor will then send your petition, the statement of arrangements for the children, a copy of your marriage certificate (if you've lost it, you can get a copy, either from the local registry office, if you still live in the area where you were married, or in person or by post from St Catherine's House, 10 Kingsway, London W.C.2), the court fee, currently £35, to the local divorce court, or to the Divorce Registry in London.

What happens next is the court sends a copy of your petition and your statement of arrangements for the children to your wife, along with an acknowledgement form, and a document explaining all the implications of the petition, and setting out her rights. She will be asked whether or not she plans to defend the petition, and if she doesn't agree with your proposals for the children, she can put forward counter-proposals of her own (she'd be advised to get legal advice before she does so), and state that she wants to take part in all discussions about the children, about property and money.

If you don't know where your wife is living, and all your own, and the courts' efforts to find her fail in locating her, so that the petition can't be 'served' on her, you can swear an 'affidavit to dispense with service', and proceed with your petition anyway.

But if you do know where your wife is, or least could find her with a little bit of effort, but lie to the court so that you can go ahead with the divorce without her being able to defend her interests, you could be in serious trouble.

In one recent case, a man divorced his wife on the grounds of five years separation without consent, and without her knowledge since he claimed she had disappeared and couldn't be traced. When he died a year later, his ex-wife, who had not disappeared at all, and could have been traced quite easily, went to court and asked for her late husband's decree absolute to be set aside. Her argument was that if the divorce was allowed to stand, she wouldn't be able to claim a generous widow's pension, and had she known about the divorce, she would have defended it on the grounds of the 'grave financial hardship' she would have suffered, unless her husband compensated her for the loss of the pension rights. The judge agreed and set aside the decree absolute, so that she was, not his ex-wife, but his widow, and could claim the pension. Had he been still alive and had not remarried, the court would have set aside the decree absolute until the financial arrangements had been sorted out. If he had remarried, the court would not have made him a bigamist by setting aside the decree absolute, but they would have made him reach the sort of financial settlement with his ex-wife that would have been reached had she known about the divorce.

If your wife does receive the papers, and decides to defend the divorce, then she has twenty-nine days in which to 'file an answer', in other words, fill in a form, setting out her reasons for defending it. She can defend it on the following grounds. First, that the claims in your petition aren't true, and therefore you are not entitled to a divorce. Second, that although the claims are true, she doesn't accept that your marriage has broken down irretrievably (the fact that *you* think it has will probably be enough for the court to grant you the divorce). Third, that you have lived together for longer than the six months allowed by the 'kiss-and-make-up' clause, and she can prove it, and, fourth, if you are petitioning on the grounds of five years separation without consent, that she will suffer 'grave financial or other hardship' as a result (see page 53).

She could also 'cross-petition', which means she could apply to divorce you instead. It's worth bearing in mind that threats to defend or to cross-petition are sometimes used as bargaining ploys to get a larger share of the family home, say, or to cement claims to the custody of the children, and that, in the end, your wife may not go through with it, and the divorce will go through undefended. But if she does decide to go ahead and defend the divorce, the case will be referred to the High Court. Eventually – and it could take a year – there will be a full court hearing, with each of you represented by barristers who will slug it out on your behalf. Almost inevitably, it will be a very unpleasant experience, with accusations and counter-accusations being hurled, and any hope of keeping the relationship civilised in sorting out the children's future will evaporate. It will also be horrendously expensive, unless you're eligible for legal aid (see page 61), costing thousands of pounds. The expense does deter some people from defending divorce. As one man quoted in an article by Mervyn Murch and colleagues, put it, 'It must be the only part of the law where you are guilty and have to prove yourself innocent – provided you can afford it! And I think that's atrocious!'

For all those reasons, the vast majority of divorces now – some ninety-eight per cent – are undefended.

If your wife decides not to defend the divorce, she has eight days in which to return the 'acknowledgement of service' form and any proposals for the children's future she may wish to make to the court. The next step is for your solicitor to apply for 'directions for trial' – a formal request for your divorce to proceed. He will then draw up an affidavit of evidence, which is a confirmation of the evidence given in your petition, the truth of which you have to swear on oath, either in front of your solicitor, or an official at the court, plus any evidence – letters and so on – that support your case.

These documents are then sent to the court – 'filed' – and your case is put on the special procedures' list, which was introduced in 1977, and is sometimes called 'divorce-by-post', since neither of you actually has to appear in court.

Although the documents about the children, property and money are sent in along with divorce petition, in terms of the legal process, they are dealt with separately from the divorce itself, so I have also dealt with them separately and in detail in Chapters 7 and 8.

The next stage in the divorce itself is that the Registrar (in effect, a junior judge) will look at all the papers, and if he decides they are in order, he will issue a certificate which will be sent to your solicitor, and pass the papers on to the judge who will set a date when he will pronounce the decree nisi in open court.

This does *not* mean that you are now divorced, or that you can remarry. What it does mean is that you can apply for a decree absolute, which does finally end your marriage, in six weeks time and it will be granted *unless* ('nisi' is the Latin word for 'unless') the court finds any reason why it shouldn't be. If you have children, the judge has to issue a certificate stating that he is satisfied with the arrangements you have made for the children (see page 78) before you can apply for your decree absolute. To get it, your solicitor applies to the court, and sealed certificates of the decree will be sent to you, and to your ex-wife as she now is. If your wife is divorcing you, and she doesn't apply for the decree absolute, then you can apply for it yourself after fourteen weeks.

Financial help with your divorce

If you can't afford the legal fees involved in divorce, there are two schemes, run by the Law Society (the solicitors' professional body) which may be able to help – legal advice and assistance (known as the green form scheme, for obvious reasons) and legal aid.

The green form scheme

Legal aid for undefended divorces was withdrawn in 1977, with the introduction of the 'special procedure', which meant you no longer had to appear in court unless your divorce was defended, but you can get up to £75's worth of legal advice from a solicitor under the green form scheme if you are petitioning for divorce, and £40's worth if you are the respondant.

It is meant to cover a solicitor's time for drawing up your divorce petition (or giving you advice once you have received your wife's petition), and writing a few letters. It is not meant to cover court appearances – an undefended divorce doesn't involve a court appearance of course, and if there is a dispute over the children or money, you can get legal aid – though in his research, Gwynn Davies from Bristol University found that a number of solicitors on the scheme did attend children's appointments (see page 78) with their clients, unpaid. Whether or not you're eligible for help under the scheme depends entirely on your financial position – what's known as your 'disposable income' and your 'disposable capital', which your solicitor will be able to work out for you there and then.

Your *disposable income* is what's left after you have deducted from your gross weekly pay – income tax, national insurance contribution, rent or mortgage repayments, travelling costs, an allowance for your wife and children if you're still living at home, or the maintenance you are paying if you have separated, insurance premiums, HP repayments and other outgoings the DHSS considers essential.

If it's less than £44 a week, you are eligible for free help under the scheme. If it's between £44 and £93, you will be asked to make a contribution, and if it's over £93, you won't be eligible.

If you are on supplementary benefit, or family income supplement, you will be automatically eligible, provided you qualify in terms of disposable capital, too.

To work out your *disposable capital*, add up all your assets including savings of all kinds, investments, possessions of value like jewellery, and the sum you could borrow against a life insurance policy, but *excluding* the value of your home, and your household furniture, your clothes, and any tools or equipment you need for your job, and an allowance for your wife and children.

If the sum you are left with is less than £655, you will be eligible. If it's over that amount, you won't.

If you use the green form scheme to help with the divorce itself, you can still apply for legal aid if you and your wife can't agree about the children, property or money. And of course, legal aid is also available if the divorce is defended.

Your eligibility for legal aid depends entirely on your 'disposable income' and your 'disposable capital'. This time, though, they have to be assessed by the DHSS, who may well call you in for an interview. It all takes time – several months – and it's important to remember that legal aid is *not* retrospective, so it will not cover any legal expenses you may have incurred before your certificate is granted. It is irritating if you are anxious to get on with the divorce, but you just have to wait.

Disposable income

The rules for working it out are the same as they are for the green form scheme, *except* you must multiply the figure you arrive at by fifty-two, to give you an annual figure, and the limits are different.

If it is less than £1,850, you will be eligible for free legal aid. If it's between £1,850 and £4,440, you will be asked to make a contribution (one quarter of the amount over £1,850, usually), and if it is over £4,440, you almost certainly won't be eligible.

Disposable capital

Again the rules for working it out are much the same as they are under the green form scheme, *except* you are not allowed anything for your wife and children, and you are allowed to exclude anything that is the subject of a dispute. If you and your wife have £1,000 in the building society and can't agree how it should be divided, then you don't include it in the total, presumably on the grounds that after the hearing it may not be yours anyway!

If your disposable capital is less than £1,310, you will be eligible for free legal aid (assuming you qualify on 'disposable income' too). If it's between £1,320 and £2,725, you will be asked to make some contribution – usually the amount you have over £1,320 – and if it is over £2,725 you will not be eligible.

The one major snag with legal aid, which many people overlook, is what is known as the 'statutory charge'. What it means is that if you get legal aid for a dispute with your wife over property or money, and you wind up with some cash as a result, the legal aid office can claim back the amount of legal aid you have had. If you wind up with less than £2,500, then you are exempt, but they can claim back anything over than amount.

Suppose you and your wife fight a long battle, both of you on legal aid, over the family home. The court decides it shall be split fifty/fifty, and since you have no children, it can be sold at once and the proceeds divided. You sell it for £23,000, pay off the mortgage and other expenses, leaving you with £8,000, to be divided equally between you. You're planning to use your £4,000 to put down on a flat, but the legal aid office wants £2,000 of it to cover your legal fees. In fact, you are allowed to keep the first £2,500, so they can only claim £1,500 but it still leaves you too little to put down on your flat. You could ask the legal aid office to postpone taking what you owe, so that you can buy your flat, and then pay them when you eventually sell it.

One very undesirable side effect of the 'statutory charge' is that it encourages people to fight for an order for 'costs' against their partner which can create enormous bitterness because having 'costs' awarded again you implies that you are the 'guilty party'.

Costs

If the judge makes an order for costs against you at the end of the hearing, it means that you have to pay your ex-wife's legal costs, as well as your own, *even if she is on legal aid*.

If you are divorcing on the grounds of two years separation with consent then it is usual for the judge to make no order for costs. After all, you have agreed mutually to end your marriage, and neither of you is at fault, so it's only right that you should pay your own costs.

If you are divorcing on the grounds of five years separation without consent, it's very unlikely that costs will be awarded either.

If you are being divorced on the grounds of adultery, unreasonable behaviour or desertion, then as the partner at fault (even though we are meant to have a 'no fault divorce' law now) costs will be awarded against you.

If your wife is on legal aid and you are paying your own legal bills, it can prove a powerful weapon in her hands. If she chooses to drag the proceedings out and get her solicitor to write to yours on every trivial detail, she knows, whatever happens, it won't cost her a penny. If she loses the battle, then the state, in the form of legal aid will pay her bill, while you will almost certainly have to pay your own. If she wins, then you have to pay her costs as well as your own, and with a long, contested custody case, for instance, costing thousands of pounds, it is a very powerful incentive for you to go along with what she wants.

If you're both on legal aid, the judge may decide that since neither of you has any money, there is no point in making an order for costs. But that isn't always the case.

Recently a couple decided to divorce after thirty years, and decided that the wife should petition on the grounds of her husband's behaviour simply because they didn't want to wait two years. Their children were all grown up, so their only asset, the family home, could be sold at once and the proceeds divided. They agreed on a sixty/forty split in the wife's favour, but she also asked for the husband to pay her costs. Since he had no capital, he would have to pay them out of his share of the house. He asked the judge if his wife's costs could be deducted from the proceeds of the house sale *before* they were divided, but the judge refused, on the grounds that he was being divorced because of his unreasonable behaviour, and therefore should pay her costs out of his own share!

Do it yourself divorce

Even if your divorce is undefended, and there are no problems over the children, money or property, it can still cost you £100 or so in legal fees, so you may decide you want to do it yourself.

You may feel, as many people do, that you will be more involved in the process this way, and can make sure that lawyers don't stir up trouble between you.

If you both agree on who shall petition and on what grounds, then you can handle the divorce yourself.

If you can also agree totally on which of you the children shall live with, and what access the other parent shall have, how much maintenance shall be paid, if any, and how the family home shall be divided, then you can handle these 'ancillary matters', too. If you *can't* agree about some or all these things, then you can still handle the divorce itself, but get professional help with the rest.

How to do it yourself

First, write to your local divorce court (see under 'county court' in the phone book) or to the Divorce Registry in London, and ask them to send you the following:

Three copies of the form 'divorce petition' (four copies if you are petitioning on the grounds of adultery, as the co-respondent must have a copy, too).

If you have children, *three* copies of the form, 'statement as to the arrangements for children'.

If you are on supplementary benefit, or family income supplement, *two* copies of the form, 'application for exemption of fees in matrimonial proceedings', which will mean you won't have to pay the court fee of £35.

One copy of the very helpful free booklet *Undefended Divorce; A guide for the petitioner acting without a solicitor.*

The court will send you all the above forms, free, though you can buy them from the specialist legal stationers, Oyez Stationery, who have shops in London, Birmingham, Bristol, Cardiff, Leeds, Liverpool, Manchester, Sheffield.

Filling in the forms

On the divorce petition, you fill in all the details that your solicitor would have filled in for you (see page 57).

On the 'statement as the arrangements for children' form, you write down with whom the children will be living, and where, giving a brief description of the home – 'two bedroomed flat', 'three bedroomed house' – where they will be going to school, how they will be supported – whether you'll be maintaining them, whether they'll be relying on supplementary benefit, and the arrangements made for access to the parent they will not be living with.

If you don't want to fill out the forms in triplicate, then do it once and get it photocopied, remembering to make a copy for yourself. Send the forms, along with your marriage certificate (or a copy, but *not* a photocopy) and the £35 court fee (unless you are exempt), to the divorce court or the Divorce Registry in London.

The court then takes over, as it would if you were using a solicitor. The next step is for the court to send you a copy of your wife's 'acknowledgement of service', plus a standard 'directions for trial' form (which simply ask for the court to deal with your case), and a standard 'affidavit of evidence' form, on which you state the reasons why you believe your marriage has broken down irretrievably, and the evidence to support it. Although you can fill in the form by yourself, you *must* sign it, and your copy of the 'acknowledgement of service' in front of a solicitor (it will cost you £1) or a court official. Send all the documents, plus any written evidence – letters and so on – to the court.

Again, the court takes over, and provided there are no problems, the date will be set for the pronouncement in open court of your decree nisi (and if you have children, for the children's appointment). Once the judge is satisfied, a copy of the decree nisi (and a copy of the judge's order concerning the children's future) will be sent to you.

All you have to do then, is get two copies of the standard form 'notice of application for decree nisi to be made absolute' from the court, fill it in and at least six weeks after the decree nisi, send them to the court. Soon after, you and your ex-wife will receive sealed certificates of your decree absolute through the post.

It is usually pretty straightforward, but remember, the moment you hit a problem – your wife changes her mind about the agreement you'd reached on the house, for instance – then do get legal advice.

7

Your Children's Future and the Law

Many fathers have been absolutely devastated to discover that, with a stroke of the pen, the courts can change their relationship with their children after divorce from that of caring parent, as closely involved in their upbringing as their mother, to little more than visiting uncle, allowed to visit them once a month, and what's more, can even send them to prison if they disobey the court order and try to see their children more often.

'I had always assumed,' said one father with a long history of access problems, 'that as a natural parent, I had a relationship with my sons that *nothing* could alter. How wrong I was!'

Most couples manage to resolve the question of the children's future between them, so that all the court has to do is approve the arrangements made. Only one case in ten is disputed, and so has to be decided by the courts, *but* the decisions made in those cases filter right through the whole system and affect the kind of arrangements solicitors suggest and the advice they give you – 'bargaining in the shadow of the law', it's been called – so that the views judges hold on the questions of children will affect the decisions about your children's future, whether your case goes to court or not.

As far as the law is concerned, there are three main decisions to be made about the children's future – which parent shall have custody, which parent shall have care and control, and what access the children shall have to the parent with whom they don't live.

Custody

Although 'custody' is often used to describe the overall responsibility for the children after divorce, it does have a more specific, legal meaning. Having custody of your children –

whether it's sole or joint – means that you have a say in their long-term future – making decisions about their education, and about religious or medical matters. It does *not* mean that the children live with you, or that you look after them on a day-to-day basis – that's care and control. One judge, revealing his own social background rather, described the difference between the two as follows: 'Custody is deciding which school the child shall go to. Care and control is packing his trunk.'

You might think that the important decision is who gets care and control and that custody doesn't really matter, a view taken by a number of judges and barristers who believe it isn't worth fighting for. But if you don't have custody (sole or joint), you are giving up virtually all your legal rights in your children. You will not be entitled to see their school reports, for example, or be invited to parents' evenings to talk about their progress. In a Court of Appeal decision in 1980, described as a 'myth' and a 'fallacy' that only the parent with custody has any rights in a child's schooling, but most education authorities don't interpret it that way, and will deny fathers without custody any information about their children.

One father fought a long battle with his daughter's school and the local education authority, and managed to wring a small concession out of them. They agreed that he could receive 'reports of a limited nature concerning the welfare of (his) child', which would be sent to him 'quarterly, co-inciding with the end of each school term.' The letter went on to give one such 'limited report' – that his daughter was happy and doing well, and was continuing to attend gym club – and that was it!

If you don't have custody, you will not be informed if your children are involved in accidents, and you will not be allowed to visit them in hospital unless your ex-wife gives her permission. According to an experienced divorce court welfare officer, it can create other unforeseen problems, too. 'I had a case where the mother, who had sole custody of the two children, died, and the local authority took them into care. It took the father months to get them out again, because he didn't have custody, and even a few months is an awfully long time in the lives of young children.'

The court can make several different custody orders. They can, for example, award custody to one parent, and care and control to the other. It was quite common ten of fifteen years ago, for the father to be given custody, while the mother had care and control, but it seemed rather silly to deny the parent who was actually bringing the children up any say in their education, so these days 'split orders' as they're called are rare. What usually happens now is that the courts award custody to the parent who has care and control – in most cases, the mother, so that the father is left out in the cold.

Judges can award joint custody – to both parents – with care and control to one of them, but they do so very rarely (in 1980, in only around three per cent of cases) on the grounds that it causes trouble. As one lawyer put it, 'When it works, it is unnecessary and when it is necessary, it is unworkable!'

Judges will usually only grant joint custody where the parents are in total agreement, and even then not always willingly, as one mother found. 'Joint custody gives my ex-husband the same legal recognition of his rights as it does to me, and it seemed the only fair way. But we had to argue for it. The judge was against it, and in the end I found myself arguing for my husband!'

But two cases that reached the Court of Appeal in 1980 and 1981 indicate that one or two judges are taking a different line. In both cases, they awarded joint custody, in spite of the fact that relations between the parents were very bad, because they believed it was the only way they could ensure that the fathers maintained their links with their children.

Many people believe that joint custody is a very good idea. 'I always encourage my clients to go for joint custody,' said a solicitor with a busy divorce practice, 'and spend a lot of time trying to persuade the other side to agree. I think it is extremely important because it helps destroy the idea of "winners" and "losers" in custody battles which does so much damage, and it prevents the parent with care and control thinking that she (or occasionally, he) has total power, and can rule the father out of the children's lives if she feels like it. It also means that fathers feel they still have a real role to play in their children's lives, which is very important psychologically, and stops children from thinking they only have one parent. And finally, it reminds the outside world – schools and so on – that the children have *two* parents who matter in their lives.

'While I do understand the judges' point that where you have a couple at war it is very hard to make a joint custody order work, I feel strongly that if joint custody was the norm, and it was made very clear that parents were *expected* to try and make it work, then the majority would try harder. At the moment, there isn't any incentive to make it work. The wife's solicitor tells her she needn't agree to joint custody, and that the court won't award it if she doesn't, then why should she make the effort?'

Groups like Families Need Fathers, and many conciliators and divorce court welfare officers would like to see joint custody orders become standard. 'It would then be up to one side to show very good reasons why the order shouldn't be made,' said a divorce court welfare officer, 'and the fact that Mum and Dad aren't speaking wouldn't qualify as a "good reason". I find that a number of Dads who were planning to fight for care and control of their children, decide not to if they can have joint custody and good access. It's the thought that they might lose their children altogether that frightens them so much.'

In a few American states, joint custody orders are now automatic, unless one parent can show good reason why it shouldn't be made in their case. A study done in California shows that even in cases where it was imposed against the wishes of one parent, joint custody causes no more problems (judging by the number of cases that come back to court) than sole custody orders. Where sole custody is awarded, it is given to the parent who is more conciliatory and more generous about the children's access to the other parent!

If you aren't awarded even joint custody, the only legal rights you retain are the right to go back to court and apply for a change in the custody order, to refuse permission for your children's surname to be changed (if your ex-wife remarries, for example), although the courts can overrule you, and to refuse permission for passports to be issued to the children.

If your ex-wife wants to take the children abroad (and that includes Scotland, Northern Ireland, the Isle of Man and the Channel Islands) even for a day, she has to ask the court's permission, not yours, although you can object to her application in court. It's unlikely that you'd want to if she's only planning to take them on holiday for a couple of weeks. But if she's planning to emigrate with them, you might object very strenuously indeed, but several recent Court of Appeal decisions suggest that it won't make any difference.

In one case, currently before the Court of Human Rights in Strasbourg, the mother remarried and her new husband took a job in South Africa, so she applied to the court for permission to take her three sons out there to live. The father, who had a very close relationship with his sons was appalled at the prospect of losing them, which is what it would have meant since he wouldn't be able to afford air fares to or from South Africa, so he opposed his ex-wife's application. The divorce court judge refused to grant her permission to go, but she took the case to the Court of Appeal, where his decision was overturned and she was given permission to emigrate. The Appeal Court judges based their ruling on a case in 1970 in which the judge had said that 'the court should not lightly interfere with such reasonable way of life as is selected by the parent to whom custody has been rightly given.' Trevor Berry, chairman of Families Need Fathers, feels that such decisions are not in the best interests of the children. 'I feel that the parent who has care and control should make a commitment to maintaining the relationship between the children and the other parent, and obviously that means not moving to the other side of the world – at least not until the children are old enough to decide whether they want to go or whether they want to stay behind with the other parent.'

If your ex-wife is foreign and wants to take the children back to her country, then the court's decision will rest on factors like how old the children are, how long they've lived in this country, what experience they've had of living in their mother's country. If the children are eight or nine, have lived here all their lives, and have only spent the occasional holiday in your ex-wife's country, it's unlikely the court would allow them to go.

If she is British, though, has remarried, and plans to take them to an English-speaking country – America, Australia, Canada, South Africa – it is very likely that the court would give her permission to take the children out of the country.

If you have good reason to suspect that your wife is planning to take the children out of the country *without* the court's permission, then you can apply immediately, either through a solicitor or in person, to have them made wards of court. What it means is that custody of the children is transferred to the High Court, so that if she tries to take them abroad without the court's permission, she can be sent to prison for contempt of court.

Obviously time is of the essence, so the children become wards of court as soon as your application is received by the High Court, even though there hasn't been a hearing. The order lasts for twenty-one days, though you can apply to have it renewed.

The moment your wardship application is received, the court will send out what's called a 'Home Office letter' to all airports and sea ports to prevent the children being taken out of the country. The court can also instruct the Passport Office not to issue passports for the children without its permission.

Care and control

Although the decision about care and control is in many ways more important than the decision about custody, since it involves where the children will actually be living, legally it is more straightforward because it can only be awarded to one parent. In the vast majority of cases, it is awarded to the mother.

You and your wife may agree that it would be best for the children to stay with her, but if you don't, and even give some thought to fighting for care and control yourself, you might be put off by your solicitor telling you that you'd be wasting your time.

'Try telling most solicitors that you want to fight for care and control of your children,' said one father, 'and you get the same response as if you had run into the back of a parked car, and said that you wanted to plead "Not guilty"!'

The reason your solicitor may well discourage you from fighting for care and control is that you don't stand much chance of getting it, and most solicitors don't like fighting what they are sure will be a losing battle.

There are several reasons why it is so often a losing battle. As I've said in the chapter on separation, perhaps the most important single factor in deciding disputed custody cases, is the *status quo* – where the children are living at the time of the hearing. If they are living with their mother, then it is very rare indeed for the courts to order them to be moved to their father. If they are living with their father at the time of the hearing though, the *status quo* isn't such a potent force, and it is nothing like as rare for children to be moved from their father's care, to their mother's.

In her pamphlet, *Child Custody: What chance for fathers?*, Susan Maidment of Keele University examined a number of Court of Appeal decisions and found that in fourteen of the nineteen cases where the children were handed over to their mother, 'there appeared to be no reasonable explanation for the custody order except favouritism to the mother.' There is little doubt that judges still believe that young children are better off with their mother, regardless of how good a parent the father might be. Appeal Court judges talk of the role which 'nature had ordained' for mothers, and of the role of the father as being only 'academic'. In one Appeal Court case in 1980, a father was ordered to hand over his three-year-old daughter to her mother, who had left home for another man when the child was only a few months old, had been taking drugs and drinking heavily, had been living in a squat, and had even attempted suicide, on the grounds that it would 'give the mother the chance of remaining stable for the daughter's sake', though the judges did say that there was 'nothing to be said against the father who was a first-rate man in every way.'

So much for the welfare of the child being 'the first and paramount consideration'!

With slightly older children – say, six to twelve – there is still a strong preference for mothers in the courts, though if you can offer a substitute mother-figure – the woman you plan to marry, or your own mother – you stand a slightly better chance. When the children are old enough to 'vote with their feet' – in their mid teens – and will live with whichever parent they want to live regardless of what the court says, the judge will usually go along with their wishes, because it's pointless to make an order that will be disobeyed.

But attitudes vary among judges when it comes to consulting children about their wishes. Some will, but others prefer not to. As Lord Justice Ormrod said, '. . . it can be extremely embarrassing to a judge when he can already see the likelihood that he will come to a decision which is adverse to the wishes of the child. One cannot get involved in an argument with an eleven-year-old child, and it is doubtful whether any useful purpose is served by interviewing a child of this age, only to make a decision contrary to her wishes. That does not do very much to reinforce her trust in adults!'

The sex of the children is also an important factor. The courts are very reluctant to give fathers care and control of their daughters, presumably because of the fear of incest. It seems rather odd, though, since no-one seems too bothered about widowers, or divorced fathers whose wives didn't want custody, left to bring up daughters, or, strangely enough, in the light of Freud's work on the Oedipus complex, about mothers and sons.

In the past, the courts have been very reluctant to split the children so that you have a daughter and three sons, they would have awarded care and control of your daughter to your wife, and therefore, of your sons, too. But there is some evidence that a few courts are dividing children between their parents if they are council tenants, because local authorities are obliged to house parents who have custody and it is the only way many fathers could set up a home where their children could come and stay. Whether the children actually live with the parent who has care and control, or whether they all live with their mother in the week, and stay with their father at weekends is up to the family to decide.

As Sir John Arnold, President of the Family Division of the High Court has admitted, there is a bias against fathers in the courts, which might seem odd at first glance, given that the judiciary is dominated by men.

'But then, you must remember what sort of background judges and barristers come from,' said a solicitor, with a lot of experience in custody cases. 'They're packed off to boarding school at seven, and only see their fathers briefly in the holidays. When their own children are born, they are young barristers, working eighteen hours a day to establish their reputations, so they see very little of them. At seven, their own children are packed off to boarding school, and they see them only briefly in the holidays . . . It's not surprising that they simply can't begin to understand the very close, loving relationship a lot of fathers have with their children.'

If you and your wife both want the children, then the only chance you have of winning is if she can't offer them a suitable home (rare these days, since the parent who gets care and control will almost always get the family home) or if you can prove she is an 'unfit' mother. In the court's eyes that means proving she is a drug addict, an alcoholic, a lesbian* or a prostitute, though many people believe that neither makes a woman a bad mother, necessarily, or that she is cruel or neglectful to the children. Obviously most mothers are none of these things, so the only options left to you are to prove that she is promiscuous, or mentally unstable and that the children will suffer as a result of living with her – in other words, go in for the kind of public character assassination which destroys any chance of keeping the relationship civilised, so that if you lose your case, it will be virtually impossible to make access arrangements work.

'I refused to blacken my wife's name in court,' said one father, who fought for care and control of his two children, 'because I don't believe she is an "unfit mother". I just believed – and still do – that the children would be better off with me, and the law does say that their welfare should be paramount. I lost, of course.'

You can appeal against the judge's decision, but do remember that what you must prove is that the judge reached the wrong conclusion on the basis of the evidence put before him. The Appeal Court judges may well feel that they would have reached a different decision, but unless they can show that the original judge's decision was wrong, or unreasonable, it will stand.

Bear in mind, too, that the legal costs of an appeal can be astronomical unless you're on legal aid – and you may not get it if the legal aid committee feels that your appeal has no chance of succeeding. Time is another factor – it can take months or even years for a case to be heard, in which time, of course, the *status quo* has become even more firmly established, and apart from the court's reluctance to disturb it, you must also consider the effects of the disruption on the children's lives.

Although the courts would never consider making an order for shared care and control, some parents and children have found that such an arrangement solves their problems very well.

* Equally, if you're a homosexual, you stand little chance of winning a contested custody case, and you may even have problems getting access.

When Bob and his wife divorced five years ago, he was awarded care and control, but since they both wanted to be closely involved in the children's lives, they decided that that the children would spend from Friday after school to Monday morning with their father, and from Monday after school to Friday morning with their mother.

'It seems to be working extremely well, and certainly both the children seem very well adjusted, and are making excellent progress at school. In fact, it was quite funny – my daughter got involved in a row with another girl at school, and was ticked off by the teacher who said she ought to make allowances for the other girl because, after all, her parents were divorced. Of course the school does know that we are divorced, but they forget because my daughter just doesn't behave like the child of a broken home.

'The children have never found it confusing, and it really hasn't created any problems. Their friends all know, and if they ring, and the kids aren't here, I just say, "They're at their mother's," and they phone them there. It's just accepted.

'I honestly think the children have benefited enormously from maintaining a permanent link with both of us, and now they're in their teens, it has positive advantages. Inevitably, tensions build up between parents and adolescents, but because we don't live together full-time, the tensions are naturally broken by the move.'

It isn't a very common arrangement, but from the evidence he has been able to collect, Dr Martin Richards from the Child Care and Development Group in Cambridge believes that it can work very well. 'Many parents can continue to share the children, and many children are able to cope with alternating between two homes.'

Once care and control has been decided, the question of access has to be decided. Access is the right of the children to go on having a relationship with the parent who doesn't have care and control, though many people tend to think of it as the other way round, which often makes the problems worse.

All the recent evidence shows how important good access is for children, and Sir John Arnold has repeatedly said that the courts are strongly in favour of it, and yet, one survey showed that in between a third and a half of cases, *no* access order was made. One argument is that the courts assume parents will work it out between them, but other people, like Dr Martin Richards, believe it shows that the courts really aren't too bothered about the relationship between the children and their other parent.

Where the courts do make an order, it's most likely to be for 'reasonable access', and leave you and your ex-wife to work out the details. If you are on reasonably good terms, you may be able to agree on regular, frequent visits – 'access' – having the children to stay for weekends – 'staying access' – and for a week or two in the school holidays – 'holiday access'.

But if you aren't on good terms, then, as one divorce court welfare officer put it, '"reasonable" access is the daftest phrase imaginable, because you are not dealing with "reasonable" people. To a Dad who's been used to seeing his kids every day, two hours once a fortnight isn't "reasonable". To a Mum who's remarried and would be happy never to set eyes on her "ex" again, two hours once a fortnight isn't "reasonable" either.

'I think the courts should make orders for "reasonable access with a minimum of X days a year", which leave it flexible enough for the people involved to arrange the time to suit themselves.'

If you feel that there are going to be serious problems with access (or if there have already been problems during the separation), you can ask the court to make a 'defined access' order, which states the time, date and place access should take place. In one extreme case, a father was only allowed to see his child for three hours once a month in the former family home and in the presence of his ex-wife and her new husband.

Obviously, defined access orders don't allow for the flexibility which is so important in making access work, but in the last resort, defined access is better than no access at all.

In a few cases, the court may make an order barring all access to the children – if you've been violent to them, for instance, or if you are a homosexual, or transvestite, though it depends largely on the judge's prejudices and the attitude of your ex-wife. Some homosexuals and transvestites are able to maintain good relationships with their children, on condition they don't flaunt their sexual proclivities while the children are around. If your application for access is turned down, it might be worth appealing.

Your children and the legal process

If you and your wife have managed to reach agreement about custody, care and control and access, then the legal process is pretty straightforward.

Once the Registrar has decided that your divorce can go ahead, he will also arrange a children's appointment for you, at which the judge will look at the arrangements you have made for the children, described on the 'statement as to arrangements for children' form you or your wife filled in, along with the divorce petition itself, and discuss them with you. Until he was declared 'satisfaction' or failing that, has declared that the arrangements are the best that could be devised under the circumstances (in practical terms, it makes no difference which he declares; it's just a legal nicety!), he will not issue the certificate you must have before you can apply for your decree absolute.

Technically, the appointment is described as 'an appointment for the *petitioner* to attend . . .', so if your wife is the one petitioning, you may not be invited along, or might even get the impression that you are not allowed to attend. Your solicitor (if you have one) may not even tell you when it is because there is no need for you to be there, since nothing will happen which hasn't already been agreed.

But you can attend, and it might be a very good idea if you do. Peter was told there was no point in him going along, and didn't think he'd bother, but at the last minute, he changed his mind and went.

'I was absolutely stunned to discover that my wife was also putting in an application to emigrate to Canada with the children. It was the first I'd heard of it, and if I hadn't been there, it might even have gone through because children's appointments are only held when the parents have agreed over the children's future, and so the implication would have been that I'd agreed to their emigrating!'

Even where there are no problems, other fathers feel it's important to go along. 'I wanted to show the judge that I still took my responsibilities as a parent seriously,' said Allan, 'and that in spite of everything, we'd managed to do something right in sorting out the children's future.'

In many cases, of course, all the judge does is rubber-stamp the agreement you have reached – one recent study done in the West country showed that the average length of children's appointments was four and a half minutes, hardly long enough for a deep, probing examination. Children's appointments are always held in private, usually in the judge's rooms, or 'chambers', but sometimes in the courtroom, closed to the press and public. (At some courts, they arrange for your decree nisi to be read out on the same day as your children's appointment, so you might find yourself herded into court with twenty or thirty other couples to hear the judge, in wig and gown, reading out all your names!)

The tone of the proceedings varies widely from judge to judge. You may find the judge in your case is very informal, and chatty, going out of his way to make you feel at ease. Or you may find him very formal, even cold. One father, who had been reassured all along by his solicitor that the proceedings would be very informal, was startled to find himself being sent into the witness box to answer the judge's questions on oath!

You may find the judge is genuinely interested in any worries or problems that still remain, and not only will he encourage you to talk about them, but may even attempt to mediate to try and resolve them. Or you may find he simply wants 'yes' and 'no' answers, and will brush aside any problems you try to raise.

When the children's appointments were established in 1977, no procedure was laid down, and the judge's role was not clearly defined, so the appointments vary from judge to judge, and you should be prepared for almost anything!

If the judge is satisfied with the arrangements, he will issue a certificate which means you can apply for your decree absolute (see page 60).

If he is not satisfied, then he will adjourn the hearing and ask the divorce court welfare officer to prepare a welfare report (see page 80). It can take several months for the report to be prepared and another appointment arranged, which obviously will hold up your divorce. At the rearranged children's appointment, having read the report, the judge will announce his decision. It would be unrealistic to alter the arrangements you have agreed on, so all he can do in extreme cases, is make a care order, putting the children into the care of the local authority, or in more marginal cases, make a supervision order which means that the welfare officer will keep an eye on the children for a while.

If you and your wife haven't been able to agree about the children's future, and are both applying for custody, care and control, then the legal process is more complicated, and what happens next depends to some extent on where you live. In the Principal Divorce Registry in London and in some areas like Bristol and Wandsworth in south west London, Registrars have introduced pre-trial reviews, meetings to which you, your wife and your solicitors are invited, and at which they attempt to mediate in the hope that you and your wife can reach agreement about the children's future without the need for a full court hearing. It may well be the first time you and your wife have talked face to face since you separated, and that may help you both to compromise and find a solution. If it doesn't work, and you can't reach agreement, then there will have to be a full court hearing.

In other areas Registrars arrange for welfare reports to be done before the first court hearing, since they're required in *all* contested custody hearings, in order to save time, but in many places, the judge will ask for the welfare report to be done at the first hearing, and will then adjourn matters for several months until it has been done.

Welfare reports

The object of a welfare report is to present as detailed a picture as possible of the options for the children's future life which involves talking to you, your wife, any prospective new partners, the children themselves if they're old enough (though what is considered 'old enough' varies from one divorce court welfare officer to another), teachers, neighbours, even child psychiatrists. If you and your wife want care and control, then the divorce court welfare officer will make a recommendation on the basis of his/her findings as to which of you should have it.

Divorce court welfare officers, like members of any other profession, vary widely in their view of their job and in their approach.

One divorce court welfare officer working in a suburban divorce court is very thorough.

'I always talk to both parents at length about their plans for the children's future – where they'll live, how it will affect the children's schooling and friendships, what arrangements they'll make if they're working, what access the children will have to the other parent, and so on. I talk to the children by themselves – I take them out to the park, or for an ice cream, and spend a bit of time getting to know them, just chatting generally to win their confidence. You *can't* just walk in, sit down and start asking them who they want to live with, especially if Mum is hovering in the kitchen, though I know what's what some welfare officers do!

'I also insist on seeing the children with both their parents in their own homes, though, again, I know some welfare officers don't. If Mum says the children don't want to see Dad, they leave it at that. If Dad only has a few hours' access a week, it can be tricky because I see no point in arriving until he and the kids have had a chance to settle down together, and that does take time. But I've got my judge well-trained. If Mum won't let Dad have a few extra hours' access so that I can make my visit, I get the judge to insist.'

Not all welfare officers are that thorough, either through lack of time, or of inclination.

'The welfare report in my case was diabolical,' said one father who wanted care and control of his three children. 'She saw me and my wife together for an hour, then saw me alone in her office. She also saw my wife alone, and saw her with the kids, but she wouldn't come and see them with me. I know the kids wanted to live with me, but the report was loaded against me.'

In another case, which Mervyn Murch reports in his book *Justice and Welfare in Divorce*, a father discovered that the welfare officer preparing the report in his case was a close friend of the man with whom his wife was living, and even she made it very clear in interviews that she felt he was very much on her side.

Other welfare officers are more concerned with the practicalities – whether your home is suitable, whether it's clean and tidy, even what kinds of books and magazines are lying around, or what posters are on the wall.

According to the Matrimonial Causes Rules which govern procedure in divorce, you have the *right* to see the welfare report in your case, and yet, a recent survey showed that a staggering seventy-one per cent of parents had *not* been shown the report. The problem stems from the fact that all reports have stamped on their covers 'Confidential report to the court. Not to be published', which many solicitors interpret as meaning it is for the judge's eyes only, and therefore won't show it to their client, though some will read out selected extracts! If you don't have a solicitor, then you are better off because the court will send you a copy of the report, direct!

If your solicitor won't let you see the report, then insist that he/she does, and quote the matrimonial causes rules! It is important that you see the report because it could contain some inaccuracies, and it could be instrumental in deciding the children's future.

If your solicitor still refuses to let you see the report, try contacting the welfare officer who did it, and asking if you can see his/her copy. Many welfare officers will be happy to show it to you, but some may be reluctant on the grounds that it might stir up trouble. Perhaps your wife has admitted in it that she is planning to remarry as soon as the divorce is finalised, something she has always denied to you in discussions over the house and money.

At the end of the welfare report, the welfare officer will probably make a recommendation about the children's future which the judge will take into consideration when he is reaching a decision. But it is only a recommendation, and the judge isn't bound to accept it, though one recent survey showed that in eighty per cent of cases, judges reached the same conclusions as the welfare officers.

The hearing will be a full court hearing, with barristers representing you and your wife, and cross-examining you in the witness box, although the court will be closed to the press and the public.

At the end of the hearing, the judge will make an order setting out the arrangements for the children, and issue the certificate you need before you can apply for the decree absolute which legally puts an end to your marriage.

8

Money, Property and things . . .

It isn't uncommon for couples whose divorce had been progressing in a reasonably amicable, civilised way to find it suddenly turning into all-out war over money and property.

One explanation could be that people are materialistic, and who gets the colour television and how much maintenance should be paid matter more than all the pain and unhappiness. But of course, it isn't that simple.

For many divorcing couples, money and property become the focus of their anger and bitterness – more socially acceptable than arguments and recriminations over the failure of the marriage itself. Since the change in the law, you can no longer make your partner 'pay' for what's gone wrong through the divorce itself, so you try to do so, literally. In many marriages, money is very much a part of the overall giving and taking, so once every other aspect of that has gone, it's hardly surprising if your instinct is to be much less generous than before.

It is also very difficult, and painful, to divide up everything you have accumulated as a couple – not so much the expensive items like stereos, but things which have no intrinsic value, but are irreplaceable. As one father put it, 'How do you divide up the photo album? You can't go through it saying, "One for you, one for me," because each snap represents something unique in your lives – the kids' first Christmas, the school play, that marvellous holiday, and so on.'

And for many people, physically dividing up their possessions – sorting the books and records into two piles – brings home to them for the first time that the relationship really is over.

As far as the courts are concerned, though, money and property, along with the children, are 'ancilliary matters', dealt with separately from the divorce itself. In most cases, the judge hands over disputes over money and property to a Registrar (in effect a junior judge; usually a solicitor), and although ideally, they should all be resolved before the decree absolute is granted, they often drag on for months, even years afterwards.

One of the main problems with decisions over money and property is that the Matrimonial Causes Act 1973, which tidied up the earlier divorce law reforms, gave the courts a completely free hand in making decisions, without any set rules, so there is no way of knowing before you go to court what the outcome is likely to be.

Before the law was changed in 1971, and there were still 'guilty' and 'innocent' parties in divorce, the courts' decisions about money and property were made with 'behaviour' very much in mind. If your wife left you for another man, for example, you would not be expected to pay her any maintenance or, rarely, only a nominal amount, and she would not be entitled to a share of the value of the family home.

But the 1971 Act did away with the concepts of 'guilt' and 'innocence' in divorce, and so 'behaviour' – unless it is what the courts call 'gross and obvious' – is no longer taken into account. If your wife leaves you for another man, you will probably wind up paying her maintenance, giving her a share in the family home, and if you have children, handing it over to her for herself and the children to live in until they have grown up. No wonder some men feel there really is no justice in divorce!

'Behaviour' can still affect the outcome of money and property disputes occasionally, but it really must be 'gross and obvious'. In one case, in 1977, the wife had refused to move into the house her husband had bought, and continued to live with her parents. He visited her there, and by the time they separated a few years later, they had two children. The court ruled that her behaviour in refusing to live with her husband was 'gross and obvious', and therefore she was not entitled to any maintenance for herself, although the children were.

Since the courts were no longer able to use 'behaviour' as the basis for deciding who gets what in most cases, new guidelines had to be found. The Matrimonial Causes Act 1973 stated that it was the duty of the courts '. . . to place the parties so far as it is practicable and having regard to their conduct, in the financial position in which they would have been if the marriage had not broken down . . .'

That clause has created enormous problems because, of course, the stark reality is that in the vast majority of cases, one wage packet or salary cannot support two households at all, let alone at the same standard of living which the family had previously enjoyed. The law does say 'in so far as it is practicable', of course, and the courts do realise in some cases that it simply isn't, and make awards accordingly. But many divorced men feel that some judges and Registrars in particular, interpret that clause as meaning that their former wives and children shall carry on living at the same standard as before, while they must fend for themselves as best they can. In one extreme case, a man appealed against the amount of maintenance he had been ordered to pay on the grounds that, having handed over the family home to his former wife and children, he couldn't afford to rent a flat for himself. His appeal was turned down and the judge asked, 'Have you a chair in your office?', and when he said he had, the judge replied, 'Sleep in that!'

Maintenance

Maintenance (or 'periodic payments' to use the correct legal term) is the amount of money paid regularly by one partner to another after divorce. In theory it can be paid by a wife to her former husband, but those cases are rare enough to get into the papers, and it is almost always the other way round.

There are other forms of financial settlement which can be made after divorce, like a lump sum payment, or secured payments (a sum invested which will provide your ex-wife with a regular income), but they are only an option if you're very rich, so maintenance is by far the most common settlement.

You and your wife may be able to agree about the amount of maintenance you should pay, if any, but in many cases, it's the courts which have to decide.

Before any decision about maintenance can be made, though, the court will need to know exactly what your financial position is. You will be asked for an 'affidavit of means' – a statement sworn by you in front of a solicitor or court official, giving details of your income, your investments, your savings and so on – along with any documents the court requires as evidence to back it up – tax returns, bank statements, building society pass books, even your statements from American Express!

Once you know that divorce is likely, then you should keep as detailed a record as you can of your financial affairs. Keep all your bank statements, get the bank to return all your cheques, keep all bills because if you can't produce them when the court asks for them, it will be much easier for your wife to claim that you are worth more than you are, and increase her demands. Besides, Registrars are more inclined to estimate up than down!

If your wife believes that you haven't declared everything – the proceeds from those jobs you did on the side for cash, for instance – she can ask the court to order 'discovery' – which means you must provide a list of all relevant documents you have or have had – and 'inspection', which means you must allow her solicitor to see them. It is not a good idea to try and hide anything because if your wife has a good solicitor, it will be easy enough for him or her to uncover it. Suppose you have had a foreign holiday, paid for out of the cash you made moonlighting so it doesn't appear on any bank statement or building society pass book. All her solicitor has to do is ask you in court how you paid for the holiday. Even if you try and bluff your way – and perjury is never a good idea – it is patently clear to the Registrar that you have had money which you have not declared. He will take a very dim view of that, and may be much less inclined to believe anything else you say.

Your wife will also have to provide an 'affidavit of means', too, and equally if you suspect she has been less than totally honest, you can apply for 'discovery' and 'inspection' too, or even be prepared to do a little detective work yourself.

In his excellent book *Divorce and your Money*, W. Harper quotes a case where the husband felt sure that his wife, who was claiming to be penniless and was on full legal aid, had some money stashed away somewhere. 'Discovery' and 'inspection' revealed nothing, but when he went through all the maintenance cheques he had paid to her while they were waiting for their case to come to court, which he had asked his bank to return to him, he found that some of them had been paid, unendorsed, into a bank account that she had not mentioned in her 'discovery' statement. The fact that they were unendorsed meant that the bank account must be hers, so he asked the bank for details of the account, and when they refused, he applied to the court for an order. A few days before the case came to court, his wife's solicitors sent him a copy of the account in question, which showed that far from being penniless, she had, at one point, over £4,000.

Incidentally, don't think that by refusing to co-operate in handing over any documents about your financial position, you will get away with paying your wife little or no maintenance. Her solicitors can apply to the court for an 'Anton Pillar' order (named after the commercial case in which it was first issued) which enables them to enter your home, and photograph any relevant papers!

How much maintenance?

Although there are no set rules when it comes to awarding maintenance, the courts do take a number of factors into account – how long you have been married, whether you both work, what pension rights your wife will lose, whether even, you are likely to inherit a lot of money. To get a rough idea of how much you are likely to have to pay, you can apply what's known as 'the one third rule'. This refers to a guideline – and it is only a guideline – laid down by Lord Denning in the case of Wachtel v Wachtel in 1973, which many judges and Registrars have used ever since.

It says, basically, that the starting point for deciding how much maintenance a wife should get, assuming the marriage has lasted more than a couple of years, should be one-third of the couple's joint income. Lord Denning felt this was fair because a man had more outgoings – for a start he would also be supporting his children, *and*, Lord Denning went on in that progressive way for which he was known and loved, 'he must get some woman to look after the house, either a wife if he remarries, or a housekeeper if he does not.'

What it means in practice is if you earn £8,000 a year (before tax) and your wife earns nothing, your total income is £8,000. One third of that is £2,666, so that is the amount of maintenance you will have to pay.

If you earn £8,000 and your wife earns £4,000, your total income is £12,000. One third of that is £4,000, the amount your wife is already earning, so you would not expect to pay her anything.

You might well think that if you have only been married a short time, have no children and have both carried on working, it is perfectly reasonable not to pay her any maintenance, and with her agreement, you could ask the court to make a consent order for no maintenance. But a recent research project revealed that twenty per cent of Registrars questioned said they would give a young, childless, working wife a full maintenance order, and only ten per cent felt she should start maintaining herself right away!

What is likely to happen is that the court will award your wife *nominal* maintenance of £1 or even 5p a week. They're the kind of awards that are often reported in a jokey way by the popular press, but they are far from a joke.

Once the court has made a maintenace order, *no matter how small* then your wife can go back to court at any time in the future, and apply for the sum to be increased to a realistic level.

In one recent case, a couple in their mid-twenties with no children divorced after four years of marriage. Their flat was sold and the proceeds divided, and since they were both working, she was awarded nominal maintenance of £1 a week. Some time later, she became pregnant by another man and had to give up work. She went back to court to apply for an increase in maintenance, and was awarded £10 a week. The ex-husband appealed, and the High Court reduced the sum to £4 a week, but even so their decision confirmed the legal principle that, financially an ex-wife remains the responsibility of her ex-husband. As a solicitor put it recently, divorce is not so much an end to your previous marriage, as a licence to marry again.

Not surprisingly, the fact that an ex-wife can claim a hefty increase in maintenance twenty or even thirty years after the divorce is a source of great bitterness among divorced men, especially those who have remarried.

'When we went our separate ways,' said one such man, 'we split everything, the proceeds of that marriage if you like – fifty/fifty. We had no children, she had a career and so didn't want maintenance – even though the court made a nominal order, she never claimed it – and I thought that was the end of that. I remarried, had a family, and then out of the blue seventeen years later, I got a letter from her solicitor saying that she had been made redundant, and the Department of Health and Social Security had told her she must claim maintenance from me. Legally, our relationship had ended years earlier, so surely it can't be right to make me financially responsible for someone who is virtually a stranger?'

Even more unfair is the situation where a couple were divorced before the law was changed in 1971 and the behaviour of the partners was taken very much into account when maintenance was awarded. In one case, the husband had been granted a divorce on the grounds of his wife's adultery in the mid 1960s, and she was awarded a token five shillings a month maintenance. Ten years later, she lost her job and at the insistence of the DHSS, went back to court to ask for realistic maintenance. Even though her husband had remarried, she was awarded one third of his income, and because he hadn't told his employers that he had been divorced, he was too afraid of the publicity to appeal, and so paid up.

If you can afford it, a lump sum payment solves all these problems, because it is a once-and-for-all payment and your wife can't come back at a future date and ask for more.

Maintenance and your pension

Another important factor the court will take into account when they are sorting out finances and property is the loss of pension rights your wife will suffer when the divorce goes through, and in these days of index-linked, contributory pensions, that can be a considerable loss.

A widow's pension is only paid to the woman to whom you are married at the time of your death, and though your ex-wife could claim a share of any lump sum also payable by the pension fund on your death as one of your dependents, the court will expect you to compensate her for the loss of the pension, either by giving her a lump sum, or a larger share of the family home.

Yvonne Moffat, chairman of the Campaign for Justice in Divorce, believes that it is unfair all round for a wife in her early or mid thirties to be compensated there and then for the loss of a pension she wouldn't have expected to get for another thirty years or so. It means that, at a time when the husband needs every penny he can lay his hands on to set up another home for himself, he is being stretched even more, financially, and unless the wife is extremely well-organised, she won't use the extra money she gets at the time of the divorce to replace her lost pension rights, so when she reaches retirement age, she may well be in financial trouble.

'We believe that a wife is entitled to a share in the husband's pension,' said Yvonne Moffat, 'but we feel it should be divided at the time of retirement or the husband's death, as they do in some countries where the widow and the ex-wife get a share of the husband's pension, according to the length of the marriages.'

One solution would be to take out an insurance policy on your own life which would provide your ex-wife with an income equal to the pension she has lost, on your death.

If you already have life insurance policies, they may well name the beneficiary as simply 'the wife'. If you have remarried, then it means your *present* wife, not the wife to whom you were married when you took the policies out. If the policy mentions your ex-wife by name, then she will be the beneficiary. You could continue paying the premiums so that she will get a lump sum on your death and so will be less likely to make a claim against your estate (see *Wills* page 98) or you could stop paying the premiums and give her the surrender value of the policy.

If you do decide to take out a policy for your ex-wife, then it's probably better to pay the premiums yourself rather than pay her extra maintenance to cover them. If she doesn't spend it on the premiums, as agreed, she could well claim against your estate after your death.

Maintenance for your children

Again, where children are concerned, there are no set rules to indicate how much maintenance the court will expect you to pay, but in *Divorce and Your Money*, W. Harper found from looking at a number of recent Appeal Court decisions that all fathers wound up paying between seven and eight per cent of their gross income for each child. If the mother was working or had some income of her own, the father paid slightly less, but the couple's joint income was *not* used as the basis for working out maintenance for children as it is for wives.

If you have four children and a non-working wife, the prospect of paying out two-thirds of your income in maintenance will be pretty daunting. But don't panic – the courts are not totally unrealistic, and sort of levelling out process takes place, and the more the children get, the less your wife will be awarded for herself, and from the cases he examined, W. Harper found that no man was paying more than forty-five per cent of his *gross* income in maintenance, though after tax, national insurance contributions and so on have been deducted, that could be over half his take-home pay.

The law says that you have an obligation to maintain all the 'children of the family', which means not only the children you and your wife had between you, or adopted, but any other child who has lived with you as a permanent member of the family – a relative's child, for instance, or your wife's children from a previous marriage if you took on responsibility for them when you married, not only if you adopted them legally. If their own father is still maintaining them, then you will not be expected to, after your divorce.

In one recent case, a man married an Australian divorcee who revealed after the marriage that she had children back home. The husband was a little surprised, to say the least, but told her to bring them over to this country to live with them, and even paid their fares. Not long after the children arrived, the marriage started to go badly wrong and divorce proceedings were started. During the first court hearing about the children's future, the woman revealed the children weren't hers, they were her ex-husband's by his previous marriage! Even so, the court ruled that the man had accepted them as 'children of the family' and therefore he would have to maintain them.

Maintenance and the low paid

If you don't earn very much, or you're unemployed, then it is obviously unrealistic for the courts to apply the one third rule, or the formula above, so another formula is usually applied.

If you are working, the court will allow you to keep the equivalent of the supplementary benefit scale rate for yourself, and any new dependents you may have (a girlfriend who lives with you, and any children you may have) *plus* your rent *plus* a quarter of your earnings. Suppose you are living alone, and earn £52 a week, after tax. The court will allow you to keep £23.25 (the current supplementary benefit rate for a single householder), *plus* £10 a week rent, *plus* £13 (a quarter of £52), making a total of £46.25. Since you only earn £3.75 a week more than that, that is the most the court would expect you to pay in maintenance.

If you are unemployed, the court will not expect you to pay

any maintenance, though they can make an order based on your *potential* earnings which wouldn't come into force until you were working again.

Incidentally, the court can also take your *potential* earnings into account if you deliberately stop working overtime, for example, or take a lower-paid job at the time of the court hearing in the hope of keeping the maintenance award as low as possible.

The same applies to your wife if she gives up her job at the time of the divorce in order to get more maintenance from you.

Once an order for maintenance has been made, it remains in force until your ex-wife either remarries, voluntarily gives up the order, or dies. If she moves in with another man, but does not marry him, the situation is not quite so clear.

A couple of years ago, the fact that she was living with someone else – cohabiting, as it's called in legal jargon – wouldn't have made any difference to your obligation to pay maintenance – a source of great bitterness among ex-husbands. These days, while there are Registrars, particularly in courts outside the larger cities who still take the view that cohabitation makes no difference, some judges will allow you to pay less maintenance to your ex-wife, provided she is reasonably comfortable in her new set-up, or even to stop paying altogether. *But* they will usually grant her 'liberty to restore' which means that if she stops living with the man, whether it is six months or ten years later, she can go back to court and claim maintenance from you.

John, who has been divorced for over fifteen years, suspected that his ex-wife was living with another man, so he wrote to her solicitors, saying he was going to apply to the court for a reduction in the maintenance he was paying. Shortly before the hearing, her solicitors wrote back, saying she had agreed to a discharge of the maintenance order, which meant an end to the maintenance payments for ever. 'I appeared before the Registrar, and presented my case, including the letter from my ex-wife's solicitors. The Registrar was extremely hostile to me, and refused to discharge the maintenance order, saying that she had been very badly advised, and awarded her nominal maintenance instead so that she can come back at any time in the future and ask for more.'

Your ex-wife can get the maintenance order registered in the magistrates' court (not in the divorce court), which means that you have to pay the maintenance to the court which then sends it on to her. The advantages from her point of view are that it is easier for her to take legal action if you stop paying.

What happens if you don't pay?

If the order is registered in the magistrates' court, your ex-wife can have a summons taken out against you for non-payment. You will have to appear in court and explain why you haven't been paying, and unless you have a very good reason – you've lost your job, for instance – then the court will order you to pay off the arrears (the amount you owe) in installments along with the regular maintenance.

If your ex-wife has to apply for supplementary benefit whenever the maintenance doesn't arrive, then provided the amount you ought to be paying is *less* than she would be entitled to on supplementary benefit she can ask the court to make the order over to the DHSS. That way, she will get the amount owing to her every week from the DHSS without fail, the court will send on the maintenance you pay to the DHSS, and if you don't pay, then the DHSS, and not your ex-wife will pursue you for the arrears.

If the magistrates' court decides that you are not paying maintenance because of 'wilful default or culpable neglect', then they can make an '*attachment of earnings order*'. This means that the amount of maintenance you have been ordered to pay will be deducted at source by your employer, along with your tax and national insurance, and paid direct to the court. Obviously, it can't apply if you are self-employed and if you change your job, the court must issue another 'attachment of earnings order' to your new employer.

Although the divorce courts can't register a maintenance order, they can issue an 'attachment of earnings order'.

'What our local divorce court has started doing,' said Jim, who has been involved in a battle over maintenance, among other things, for the last five years, 'is issuing an 'attachment of earnings order' but suspending it, on condition you pay maintenance direct to the court – which has the same effect as registering the order in a magistrates' court.

'This happened to me, even though the law states quite

clearly that the courts can only make an attachment order if the reasons for non-payment are 'wilful default and culpable neglect'. I stopped paying because I lost my job, and when I did get another one, I wasn't earning enough to pay off the arrears and start paying maintenance again.

'When I appealed against the order, all the court would do was suspend it as long as I paid maintenance directly to them every week. I asked if I could pay monthly, as I get paid monthly, but they said no. They won't accept cheques, so I have to send a money order every month which costs me money.

'I'm now self-employed, so the threat of an attachment order doesn't worry me, but I'm still fighting it because of the principle. For one thing, it's degrading – it makes it look as though you can't be trusted, and for another, it takes away all initiative. If you're put on short time, or your overtime is stopped, it makes no difference – they still want the same amount.'

If you deliberately flout an 'attachment of earnings order' by changing your job without telling the court, or by giving up work altogether, then the court can send you to prison for a maximum of six weeks. Around 3,000 men go to prison each year for non-payment of maintenance, a number of whom deliberately withold it in protest at being denied access to their children. The irresponsible man who simply wants to avoid paying can usually manage to disappear without too much difficulty.

What happens if you can't pay?

If your circumstances change, then rather than wait until arrears build up and you are summonsed to appear in court, you can go back to court yourself and ask for a 'variation' – a change in the amount of maintenance you have been ordered to pay.

If you have lost your job or have been forced to take another job with lower pay, you will probably get a sympathetic hearing. If you have remarried, and find the extra responsibility of a second wife and family hard to cope with financially, then up to a couple of years ago, you could have expected pretty short shrift from the judge or Registrar, on the grounds that your first wife and children must come first and if you can't maintain two families you shouldn't have embarked on the second marriage.

Some judges and Registrars still take that view, but there have been a number of cases recently which indicate that the courts are taking a more realistic view and treating the interests of both sets of children as equal, a trend which many lawyers believe will grow over the next few years.

Equally, your ex-wife is free to go back to court and ask for a 'variation' – in her case, an increase in the amount of maintenance you pay – if her circumstances, or yours, change.

According to the Campaign for Justice in Divorce, it's not uncommon for an ex-wife to go back to court when her ex-husband remarries and apply for an increase in maintenance on the grounds that with two salaries coming in (assuming the second wife works, of course), his financial circumstances have improved and therefore he can afford to pay her more.

Technically, the courts cannot force your second wife to reveal her assets and income if your ex-wife is asking for more maintenance, but there have been some contradictory High Court rulings, and some judges and Registrars may still ask her for an 'affidavit of means'.

Even if they don't, there are other ways of getting the information. *You* can be asked in court what your second wife earns, or your ex-wife's solicitors can make such an exaggerated assessment of her worth that the only way to disproving it is to tell the truth.

There is nothing to stop your ex-wife going back to court at regular intervals to ask for a 'variation'. She will probably be eligible for legal aid to cover her costs, but if she wins, the court will probably order you to pay them as well as your own. The total legal fees in a defended variation hearing could be £1,000!

But it isn't just the expense that can create so much bitterness in second marriages, as Yvonne Moffat, of the Campaign for Justice in Divorce points out.

'Before the hearing, there will have been three or four months of bargaining through affidavits and solicitors' letters, which is extremely stressful, and it is very hard to think about anything else. And there is really no way round it – if you try to avoid the aggravation by simply agreeing to your ex-wife's demands right away, assuming you can afford to – then she and her solicitor will think they've asked for too little, and will come back for more, if not this time, then next time.

'Where you have a *vindictive* ex-wife – not one who just needs the money – who is using variation of maintenance applications to get back at her husband, it isn't surprising that so many second marriages break down.'

Maintenance of ex-wives is second only to problems over children as a source of anger and bitterness among divorced men. Some feel it is totally unjust that they should have to go on supporting a woman who chose to end the marriage, not because they were cruel or adulterous but because the spark had gone out of it. Others feel deeply resentful that it can go on for ever. As one man put it, 'In my blackest moments, I wish I had killed my wife. I'd have served twelve or fifteen years in prison, but then it would have been over, and I would have been free. As it is, it is a real life sentence.'

In 1982, both the English and the Scottish Law Commissions produced proposals to change the law where maintenance is concerned.

The Scottish Law Commission suggested that ex-wives should receive maintenance for three years after divorce, and then should support themselves, although there would be exceptions where it was unrealistic to expect a woman to be independent.

The English Law Commission also recommended a change in the law to encourage 'a smooth transition from marriage to independence', except where grave hardship would result, though it did not recommend any time limit. It also stressed that the interests of the *children* should be the court's overriding concern.

A number of groups, from the Campaign for Justice in Divorce to Families Need Fathers and Gingerbread, the single parents' self-help organisation, broadly welcomed the proposals. Gingerbread at its AGM in 1979 agreed that fathers should continue to maintain their children after divorce, but not their ex-wives, on the grounds that you can't press for equal opportunities *and* support measures that keep women dependent on men financially. Other groups don't agree. The National Council for One Parent Families believe that while women's earnings are still so much lower than men's, and while the level of unemployment is so high, ex-husbands should go on maintaining their ex-wives.

In December 1981, it was announced that, following the Law Commission reports, the government would be bringing in new legislation to change the law on maintenance in the 1982/83 session. There were no proposals in the Queen's Speech but in November 1982, Leo Abse, chairman of the all-party committee on divorce law reform announced plans to bring in a Private Members' Bill (with government support) to reform the law on maintenance along the lines the Law Commission had suggested. But the proposed bill also suggested re-introducing the concepts of 'guilt' and 'innocence' when it comes to making maintenance awards, something *not* recommended by the Law Commission. Many people who were all in favour of abolishing the concept of 'maintenance for life', felt that re-introducing 'guilt' and 'innocence' was a backward step, and in fact the bill fell before its second reading in February 1983.

One of the major problems has always been that no-one knows how well – or badly – the present system of maintenance works in practice, because no statistics are kept. The only piece of research to be published to date, done in 1982 by Mavis Mclean of Wolfson College, Oxford, revealed that only six per cent of the women interviewed relied on maintenance as their main source of income, although the number of ex-husbands concerned who were low-paid, or unemployed, and therefore unable to pay maintenance, was considerably higher than in the population generally.

Maintenance and tax

From the day you separate officially, you and your wife are treated as individuals by the tax man, though you will continue to get the married man's allowance for the remainder of that financial year. From then on, once the divorce is finalised, you get a single person's tax allowance only, though you can claim tax relief on maintenance paid to your ex-wife and children under certain conditions. If you pay maintenance *voluntarily*, then you will not be entitled to tax relief, so even if you and your wife are on the best of terms, and agree between you on the amount you should pay, do get the court to make a 'consent order' for the amount you have agreed. That way, it is legally enforceable, and so you can claim tax relief on what you pay.

As far as the inland revenue is concerned, there are two types of awards – large maintenance awards and small maintenance awards. If you are paying a large maintenance award (currently over £33 a week for your ex-wife and £18 for each child) then you must deduct the amount of tax due on the money, send it to the inland revenue and give the balance to your ex-wife. If she doesn't pay tax, then she can claim back the tax you have paid on the money. You can then deduct the full amount from your earnings when you are assessed for tax.

Suppose you are paying your ex-wife £60 a week under a court order. You deduct the tax due – £18 at thirty per cent – sent it to the inland revenue, and pay the balance – £42 – to your ex-wife.

If she doesn't pay tax, she can claim the £18 back, so that she gets the full £60, and you can deduct the full £60 from your taxable income.

If it is a small maintenance award (currently under £33 a week for your ex-wife and under £18 for each child), then you pay the full amount to her direct. If she is liable for tax, she then pays tax on the money and you can claim the full amount against your taxable income. The thinking is, presumably, that if the award is small, it is unlikely that the wife will be paying tax, and therefore it is a waste of time and money for the tax to be paid and claimed back.

It is also a good idea, from the tax point of view, to make any maintenance for your children payable to them *direct*. It then forms part of their income, not your ex-wife's, and just like everyone else, they are entitled to the single persons' tax allowance, currently £1,600. Unless you pay them more than that, there will be no tax payable on the money, and everyone benefits – except the taxman!

Wills

Getting divorced doesn't automatically revoke any will you may have made, so if you don't remarry, then you should make a new will. If you do marry again, any will you have made previously *is* automatically revoked, though even if you make a new will leaving everything to your second wife and children, there is no guarantee that they will get it.

Under the Inheritance Act 1975, the courts have powers to overturn wills and divide up estates as they see fit, so if your ex-wife has not remarried and did not receive a lump sum payment from you when you divorced (getting the family home doesn't count!), she can claim a share of the estate you and your second wife built up together after the divorce, and stands an excellent chance of getting it. In Maggie Drummond's excellent book *How to Survive as a Second Wife*, there is a case where a man died leaving £50,000 to his second wife and their twelve-year-old daughter. His first wife, divorced twenty years earlier, claimed £10,000, and in an out-of-court settlement, got it. The case dragged on for over two years, the legal fees were already £7,000, which would have to come out of the estate – in other words, what was left for the second wife and her daughter – and her solicitors advised her to settle because if the case did come to court it was very likely that the first wife would win.

Another woman was advised recently to go on paying £10 a month maintenance to her late father's ex-wife whom he had divorced after a brief, childless marriage forty-five years earlier, so that she wouldn't realise he had died, and wouldn't claim against his estate.

If you do remarry, the only way of protecting your second wife is by making sure that as much of your property as possible is in joint names, since your ex-wife can't claim against your second wife's property. If you have children from either marriage, make sure they are taken care of by some form of special investment. It's worth getting professional advice from an insurance broker, or if you have a good relationship with him, your bank manager.

Dividing up the assets

These days, most couples' major asset is the family home, but the decision about who gets what are complicated by a number of other factors, so it is better dealt with separately later on.

As for the other assets, as a general rule, anything bought by either of you, or jointly, and intended for the benefit of the family as a whole is treated as a family asset, and divided between you.

Anything you bought for yourself, or brought with you into the marriage – records, books, pictures, cameras, and so on –

and any gifts made to you personally during the marriage are yours.

When it comes to capital – building society deposits, savings, shares, even money you may have inherited during the marriage – it is considered a family asset and will be divided between you. If it is in your name, the 'one third rule' will apply and your wife will be able to claim at least a third.

Furniture and equipment like washing machines, is usually considered along with the family home.

The family home

As well as being your greatest asset, it is also the place where you have all been living, which complicates matters enormously.

If the house/flat is in joint names, then a fifty/fifty split is usually considered fair, especially if you have both worked and contributed to the purchase of the house. If your wife did not contribute financially, and the marriage has lasted only a short time, the court may still decide she is entitled to a third of its value.

If the house/flat is in your name only, then the court will consider the contribution your wife has made, either financially, or by staying at home and looking after the home, and will use the one third rule as a basis for awarding her a share. It makes no difference if you owned the house outright before you married, or even if it has been in your family for generations.

If you have no children then either way, it is relatively straightforward. Either you sell the property and divide the proceeds between you or, if one of you wants to stay, you will have to raise the money – by increasing or extending the mortgage perhaps – to buy the other out. If you can't agree which of you should live in it, the court will almost certainly allow whichever of you is living there at the time of the hearing to stay on (see *Separation* page 18).

If you agree that your wife shall stay on, then you could lose out. In a recent case, a couple with no children divorced after a few years of marriage and agreed that she would stay in the flat, and pay him fifty per cent of its value. The wife's boyfriend moved in, and when the husband pressed for his half share, the judge decided that since the wife would have to sell the flat in order to pay the husband his share, he would award him only one-third of its value, after all.

If the home is in your name only, you may find that your wife's solicitor holds up the decree absolute until you have finalised the settlement. The reason is, technically speaking, once the decree absolute is granted, your wife is no longer legally your wife, and so you could apply to the county court to have her evicted from your home. In practice, of course, it is highly unlikely that the county court would grant you such an eviction order, but some lawyers prefer to do everything by the book.

If you have children, the situation is much more complicated. The court may well divide the home between you, fifty/fifty, or sixty-seven/thirty-three *but* whichever of you is to look after the children – almost certainly your wife – will be allowed to live in it until they have grown up and left home – which could be in ten, or even seventeen years' time. Only then can the house be sold, and the proceeds divided up, so the reality for many men, is that they lose their home and any chance of buying another one.

'There's an old saying that an Englishman's home is his castle,' said a divorce court welfare officer, 'but I think these days they should add "until his wife decides she wants a divorce".'

Alternatively, the court may decide to award the house to your wife outright, to compensate for loss of pension rights and/or in exchange for reduced maintenance payments, or no maintenance at all. If there is a mortgage on the home, and you are to go on paying it as part of the settlement, try to persuade your wife to take higher maintenance and make the repayments herself. That way you can claim tax relief on the maintenance you pay, *and* on a mortgage for yourself, if you're able to buy another home, whereas you can't claim tax relief on two mortgages.

If you have any choice in the matter, it is hard to say which is the lesser of two evils where the family home is concerned. If you agree to wait until the children have grown up before the house can be sold and you can claim your share, then your capital is tied up for years, and you may find it impossible to buy another home. And there is another possible snag. There have been cases in recent years where ex-wives have gone back to court after the children have grown up and left home, claiming that the upheaval of a move at this stage in their lives would be too distressing, and the courts have ruled that they can stay in the house until they either remarry or die.

The second alternative – handing over the home outright to your wife – has the advantage of certainty – you won't fall into the trap of banking on capital which, in the end, you may not get after all! The fact that you'll pay less maintenance may make it slightly easier to set yourself up in a home of your own. Do bear in mind, though, that the transfer of the house is a once-and-for-all transaction and is not affected by your wife's remarriage, while maintenance payments are.

It is not unknown for a wife who is planning, secretly, to remarry as soon as the divorce is finalised, to suggest to her husband that she has the house in exchange for claiming no maintenance – maintenance which she would stop getting almost instantly, when she remarried.

In one recent case, the wife denied she was about to remarry, got the family home in exchange for no maintenance, then immediately married her boyfriend and gave him a half share in the house. Her ex-husband went back to court, on the grounds that his ex-wife had committed fraud, and the judge found in his favour. He was awarded one-third of the value of the family home, though he wouldn't be able to realise it until his eight-year-old son, who was living with his ex-wife, had grown up and left home.

According to a number of fathers, the best solution to the problem is to persuade your wife to sell the family home, provided it's worth enough, divide the proceeds and buy yourselves a less expensive home each.

'But naturally,' said one man with a degree of cynicism, 'it depends on getting her to agree before she falls into the clutches of a solicitor! Once she's been told she can get the whole lot, you've got no chance!'

What happens if you don't own your home?

Private rented accommodation

If you have no children and the tenancy is in both your names, then you both have the right to go on living there, and if you can't agree on who should leave, it is unlikely that the court will make the decision for you.

If the lease is in your name, then you have the right to stay, and your wife will have to leave. If it is in her name, then you will have to go.

If you have children, and the tenancy is in both your names, then the court will order the tenancy to be transferred to whichever of you is going to look after the children.

If it is in your name, and your wife is going to look after the children, the court will order the lease to be transferred to her, *provided* the landlord agrees. Even if there is a clause in your tenancy agreement which says that the lease cannot be assigned (transferred) *without the landlord's consent*, he cannot withold his consent, as long as your wife will be a 'reasonable' tenant – in other words, if she will pay the rent, and has no history of rent arrears.

If the tenancy simply states that the lease cannot be assigned, the landlord cannot be forced to agree.

Council, or housing association accommodation

If you have no children, and the tenancy is in both your names, then under the 1980 Housing Act, you both have security of tenure, which means you both have the right to stay. If you can't agree which of you should leave, it is unlikely that the court will make the decision for you. If you have been violent, your wife may be able to get an exclusion order (see page 20) but as you have no children, she will not be able to have you excluded from the home simply because it is unbearable for you both to go on living there. If you can show that either of you is suffering mental or physical ill-health as a result of having to live under the same roof, the council may offer to rehouse one of you, though you would be pretty low down on the list of priorities.

If the lease is in your name, your wife will have to leave, and if it is in hers, you will be the one who has to go.

If you have children, and the tenancy is in both your names, then under the 1980 Housing Act, you both have the right to stay, and only the divorce court can order the tenancy to be transferred to whichever of you is going to look after the children.

What it means is that you both have the legal right to stay in the home until your divorce is finalised, *unless* your wife applies to the court for an exclusion order, which would force you to leave *even if you have not been violent or threatened violence* (see *Separation* page 19).

If the tenancy is in your name only, and your ex-wife is going to look after the children, or if the tenancy is in her name, then you will have to leave. You then become a single homeless person, and the local authority has no obligation to offer you somewhere else to live. Some local authorities are more helpful than others, though, so it is worth finding out what your chances are.

9

Going It Alone

If the court awards you care and control of your children, then it is not the end of the story, but very much the beginning because divorce – and its consequences – is not an *event* in your own, and your children's, life, it is an 'ongoing situation', if ever there was one! How you cope with being a single parent depends to a large extent on the circumstances leading up to the decision that you would look after the children. If you and your ex-wife were able to agree that the children would be better off with you, then you will have had time to adjust to the idea, and to start organising your life, and you will be free from the sort of stress and bitterness that are an inevitable result of a fiercely contested court battle over the children's future. As one father put it, 'If you're involved in all-out war over the children, then all you think about is winning. Actually winding up with a couple of kids who need feeding and clothing and generally running round after, comes as one hell of a shock!' Obviously, if you've wanted the children all along, you'll find it easier to cope than you would if your ex-wife simply walked out on you all, leaving you with no choice in the matter.

The first major decision you'll have to make is whether to carry on working (assuming you have a job) or whether to give up, for a while anyway, and devote yourself to bringing up your children. It isn't an easy decision, and there are a number of factors you should bear in mind. For a start, there's the crucial question of money. Despite popular prejudice, supplementary benefit will keep you on, or fractionally above the poverty line, so unless you are in a very low paid job, giving up work will mean a sharp drop in your income. Will you be able to manage?

If you are buying your house on a mortgage, will you be able to keep up the payments? Until 1983, you could have changed to a less expensive option mortgage, but changes in the way tax relief is paid on mortgage repayments means that in some ways, all mortgages are option mortgages anyway, so that no longer applies. You could ask the building society to accept repayment of the interest only for a while (which the Department of Health and Social Security will usually pay, unless they consider the house too expensive for your needs), or you could take a lodger. The terms of your mortgage may say you can't, but if your local branch manager is sympathetic, he may be prepared to turn a blind eye.

If you still can't afford to keep up the repayments, then you could sell up and buy somewhere cheaper (some building societies will give you a mortgage if you are on supplementary benefit), or if that's not possible, move into rented council accommodation, though do bear in mind, if you wind up with some capital after the sale, it may affect your eligibility for supplementary benefit. It's worth talking to someone from your local Housing Advice Centre or welfare rights office before you make a decision.

The local authority does have an obligation to house you as a single parent, but the policy of many housing departments is to offer single parents the flats and houses that no-one else wants because they are run-down, or in bad areas. Many of them also have a 'one-offer only' policy, which means what it says – if you turn down the flat they offer you, they won't offer you anything else, so you're on your own. Again, it's worth getting advice before you make the decision. If you want to go on working, who'll look after the children? If they're in their teens, that isn't such a problem, but what if they are under five, or at primary school – who's going to look after them all day, or between four o'clock and the time you get home and in the holidays?

And then there is the question of isolation. For many men, work is also their social life – colleagues are also mates – and so if you give up your job, you're losing that side of your life, too.

And of course, you also have society's attitude to contend with. A recent survey about single parents revealed that less than a quarter of people interviewed thought that single mothers should go out to work, but *over three-quarters* felt that single fathers should! It's an attitude that seems pretty deep rooted in social work and the law. There was that infamous case a few years ago where the judge took a three-year-old girl away from her father who had cared for her since his wife walked out two years earlier, and handed her back to her mother on the grounds that a man shouldn't 'waste' his abilities on parenting, but should use them to earn a living!

What happens if you decide not to work?

First of all, you must go to your local social security office, and apply for child benefit, one parent benefit (both of which you're entitled to, whether you're working or not) and supplementary benefit. While you're on supplementary benefit, child benefit and one parent benefit will be deducted from it, but it's still worth applying, so that you'll get them if you do start work again.

Don't be surprised if the DHSS official on the other side of the counter makes it very clear that, like most people, he/she feels that you should go out to work. You may even be given the impression that you are not entitled to supplementary benefit, and that you have no alternative but to hand the children over to their mother, or put them into care. *That is not true* – you *are* entitled to supplementary benefit if you are bringing up children single-handed, so insist on it as your right.

Many single parents, of both sexes, find the DHSS unhelpful, to say the least, and one of the most common complaints is that the officials never tell claimants about all the different benefits they may be entitled to.

'I don't know even now what I'm entitled to,' said Derek, who's been bringing up his four children single-handed for six years. 'I have to rely on their jurisdiction if I want something. I don't know whether I'm entitled to claim it, so I don't know whether I'm going down there on false pretences. I think you should know all your rights, or be issued with a pamphlet stating how much you're allowed to claim. As it is, the begging and pleading you have to do down there sometimes is very humiliating.'

If you want to know exactly what you're entitled to (and there are literally dozens of different benefits you might be able to claim), then contact your local welfare rights office, or Gingerbread group (they'll be in the phone book, or if not, contact their head office in London) or the National Council for One Parent Families in London (addresses on page 152). They produce all sorts of useful leaflets, setting out what's on offer and how to set about claiming.

Even if you do manage to find your way successfully through the welfare rights maze, and wind up with everything you're entitled to, you will still find it a struggle to make ends meet. Unless you've always been closely involved in running the home, you won't be used to shopping and cooking, and it will harder for you to cope than it would be for a single mother. If you're not an experienced cook, you'll probably rely to a large extent on convenience foods – frozen fish fingers, bought cakes, take-away fried chicken, which are most expensive than their home-made equivalent.

You can quickly learn a bit of basic cooking, but if there are some things you can't master, then perhaps members of your local Gingerbread group will be able to help. It is a self – and mutual – help group, and you may be able to find other single parents who are happy to swap a bit of baking or mending for decorating, or heavier household repairs.

Many single fathers, at the beginning anyway, feel they have to do everything by the book. 'When my wife first left us,' said Ron, who's bringing up his two daughters on his own, 'it used to take me five hours to do the ironing. I even used to iron the girls' school knickers and socks. Not any more!'

When you were given care and control of your children, the court may have made a supervision order, which means appointing a divorce court welfare officer to keep an eye on you and the children, and help with any problems that arise. Some fathers resent what they see as 'interference', and feel that officialdom is just waiting for them to make a mess of things. Others find their welfare officer helpful and reassuring. And reassurances that they are doing a good job in bringing up their children is something that most single fathers feel they need. As Patrick put it, 'I think you need a bit of saying "The kids are being brought up all right". I mean, it's all right your own mum saying it, but I'd like someone who knew about kids to say "Well, your kids seem to be all right!"'

Without a doubt, one of the major problems facing single fathers who give up work, according to a study done in Nottingham by Tony Hipgrave, is isolation. When you give up your job, you also give up regular contact with your mates, and even if you meet for a drink sometimes – assuming you can afford it, and get a babysitter – you may well find that you don't have much in common any more. They're still bothered about the threat of redundancies, while you're more bothered about the price of school shoes. You may find, too, that they're a bit uncomfortable with you, that they feel what you're doing is a bit odd.

But if you don't keep in touch with old friends, what are the alternatives? Women in the same position usually know other Mums, single parents or not, through their children, and so it's not that difficult to make friends. But even if you do meet some Mums through your children, it's not that easy just to pop in for coffee and a chat, or to ask for advice, as several lone fathers have found.

'There was a family living just down the road with kids the same age as mine more or less. I got to know them gradually, and she invited me to bring my youngest to tea one afternoon, to play with her youngest. We went a few times, and when the little ones both started at play-group, I carried on popping in now and again. Next thing I know, the husband is ringing the doorbell – would I mind not popping in during the day. *He* knew there was nothing going on, but the neighbours were talking, and it was a bit awkward.'

You may be luckier and make friends with people who know what the neighbours think, and don't care!

One answer to the problem could be to join your local Gingerbread group. With one-in-six single parent families headed by men, there is a good chance of meeting other men in your situation.

You might be put off by the prospect of groups whose members have nothing in common but their problems, but they can be a very good place to start. For one thing, unlike many other organisations, they do understand that it's impossible for you to go anywhere unless there's someone to keep an eye on the children, so they arrange baby-sitting circles, or organise group activities for children.

Overall, the advice offered by men who are, or have been, single fathers, is to keep your job if you possibly can. 'Obviously, if it's a choice between giving up work or having your kids put into care, there *is* no choice. But otherwise, I'd say keep your job, no matter how hard it is to manage. If I'd been stuck in the house full-time, I'd have gone mad, and that wouldn't have done me, or the kids, any good at all.'

What happens if you decide to go on working?

If you keep your job, then you'll find yourself facing the problems that the vast majority of working mothers complain of – discrimination in promotion, or even in getting a job at all, because in employers' eyes, 'parent' means 'unreliable'. If the children get measles, you'll have to stay home to look after them, and you won't be able to dash off to the Liverpool branch for a fortnight, or work late at a moment's notice.

What it all boils down to, of course, is the appalling lack of decent child-care facilities for working parents – of both sexes.

If your children are under five, you might be able to find them a place in the local council day nursery, open from about 8 a.m. to 6 p.m. But places are extremely hard to get, especially with all the spending cuts, and go to children with the highest priority. In many areas, single working parents, especially fathers, are given top priority, but unfortunately, you can't assume that your children will automatically get a place. Your local social services department will be able to give you a list of the nurseries in your area.

A few enlightened employers provide creches for their employees' children, but again, in the present economic climate, facilities like that tend to be regarded as expendable.

There will probably be state nursery schools in your area, but the emphasis is on 'school' rather than 'nursery', and they only operate part-time – usually three hours in the morning or the afternoon – so they aren't a solution to the problems of the working parent. The same is true of playgroups. They're invaluable if you are at home with the children full-time, because they give you a few hours' break from each other, but they won't enable you to work.

Alternatively, you could leave your children with a registered childminder – a woman who has been approved by the local authority to look after a specified number of children in her own home during the day.

The local authorities' approval depends more or less entirely on the physical environment – the size of the woman's home, the absence of health hazards, like unguarded fires, or damp – because the legislation was introduced after a number of scandals about rows of babies being kept in conditions of almost Dickensian squalor.

Some childminders see their job only as keeping their charges fed, clean, warm and safe, but others do try and provide some mental stimulation as well – something the National Childminders' Association is trying to encourage.

However desperate you are, don't resort to an *un*registered childminder. Provided the woman's home reaches the required standard, there is no disadvantage in being registered. If her home *isn't* up to standard, then you wouldn't want to leave your children there anyway.

The local social services department will have a list of registered childminders in the area. The amount they charge varies, depending on where you live, but you can expect to pay between £12 and £25 a week. Don't forget that as a single father, you can claim tax relief on your child-care costs – something single mothers can't do, which is grossly unfair!

You may be lucky in having a relative or friend living close by is willing to look after the children while you're at work. In many ways it's an ideal solution because you'll have no qualms about leaving the children there, and they'll already know the person who's looking after them. If your own parents volunteer to help out, do bear in mind that people in their sixties and seventies don't always have the energy or patience to cope with small children full-time, so it's probably best to think of it as a short-term, rather than a long-term solution.

With friends and neighbours who are at home looking after their own children, you have to be a little bit careful. You will probably want to put the arrangement on a proper footing, paying for your children's food and contributing towards heating and so on, but technically speaking anyone who receives payment for looking after someone else's children should register as a childminder. Also, once it becomes a business arrangement, you lose the flexibility you had when it was just a favour. Your neighbour or friend may be embarrassed to tell you that they don't want to carry on, so you have to be very sensitive and ask every now and then if they're still happy with the arrangement.

If you have the room, and the money, you could employ a nanny, or if the children are older, a housekeeper, but they are expensive, it's not easy to find the right person, and even if you do, it always takes some adjusting to having a stranger living under your roof.

A cheaper alternative is to advertise locally for a woman

whose own children have grown up and left home, who'll come in for a few hours every afternoon so that there's always someone there when the children come home.

If you can't afford to do that, then it might be worth thinking about sharing your home with another single parent – a single mother perhaps, who could look after both sets of children while you go out to work – and sharing the bills. An agency called *Singlehanded Ltd* (address on page 153) will put you in touch with other single parents for a fee. They ask you to fill in a very detailed questionnaire about yourself, and your attitudes to many things, including how children should be brought up, so they can put you in touch with like-minded single parents. They don't guarantee that you will get on, but at least they can avoid putting you in touch with people who hold diametrically opposed views!

If you get on well when you meet, perhaps you could try it out for a couple of weeks in the holidays before you commit yourself. Of course, it doesn't work for everybody, but where it does, there are lots of advantages besides the more obvious financial ones. Many single parents find their relationship with their children becoming very claustrophobic, and just having another adult in the house who can take the pressure off you from time to time, and to whom you can have a good moan sometimes, can be a great help.

Once the children start school, the problems don't disappear, they simply change. Unless you're a teacher and work the same hours as your children, then you'll have to make arrangements for them after school and in the holidays. With the growing number of single parents and families where both parents have to work, there is at least a recognition of the need for more facilities. Some schools now stay open after hours, organising sport and other leisure activities, and some local authorities organise holidays schemes, using schools' facilities, but again, they are often the first to fall victim to spending cuts. Gingerbread has set up a number of schemes in various parts of the country (contact your local group, or the head office for details) and other voluntary groups run projects too, so it's worth checking with your local social services or welfare rights group if there is anything going on near you. If there's no official help on offer, you may find friends and neighbours willing to help –

after all, having the children for a couple of hours after school isn't the same as having them all day, every day, and many parents who've come to dread the familiar holiday cry, 'I'm *bored*!', will welcome another child or two for their own to play with.

If you have to leave home very early in the morning, you might be able to persuade your local social services to provide a home help who would come in to get the children up, give them their breakfast and see them off to school. If you start work that early, then chances are you'll be home when the children get in from school. If you run into major problems – you're ill, or the arrangements you've made for the children in the holidays have suddenly collapsed – the social services may be able to help. It varies from area to area, but with all the spending cuts, many departments are only able to deal with 'life or death' emergencies, and if you want anything done, you must be prepared to keep on at them until they do respond. It can often be impossible to get just that little bit of help from social services that would make all the difference. As one director of social services in a large northern city put it, 'If you've got a massive big problem, we've got a massive big answer!' If you are in serious difficulties, the social services may offer to take the children into care, temporarily, but before you agree, *get advice* from your local Law Centre, or from the National Council for One Parent Families or the Family Rights Group (addresses on page 153). There have been cases recently where parents who have put their children voluntarily into care, have found that the local authority has had them fostered, and it's impossible to get them back again.

As if all the practical difficulties weren't enough to cope with, you may well find there are emotional problems, too. Again, it will depend on how the children came to be living with you. If the arrangements were all worked out between you and your ex-wife, and she sees the children as often as she – and they like – then chances are, after an initial period of adjustment, there won't be many problems.

But if there was a long, bitter battle over care and control, which is still going on over access, then there will be problems.

As we've seen in the chapter on access, in the vast majority of cases, children need a good relationship with both their parents, regardless of how the parents feel about each other. Most custodial parents are women – about eight out of ten – and some behave extremely badly over access, but then so do some custodial fathers.

Don't try and prevent your children from seeing their mother, and don't make them feel guilty or disloyal if they want to. In fact, encourage them to see her. It won't be easy, but in the long-term, it will pay dividends for all of you.

If your ex-wife doesn't keep in touch with the children, you may well find they become very clinging. They won't want to let you out of their sight, and if you have to go, they will want you to account for your every move. It's perfectly understandable – they've lost one parent, something they never dreamt could happen, so in their minds, there is no reason why they couldn't lose you, too.

'Once, about six months after my wife had left,' said Roy, who's bringing up his seven-year-old son and six-year-old daughter, 'I called next door for a cup of coffee. I must have been in there for about half an hour, and when I came home, I found them sitting on the stairs, crying their eyes out because they thought I'd left them. It nearly made me cry!'

Like many single parents, you might find that trying to be both father and mother to the children isn't easy. Discipline can be a problem. How can you smack a child if you're the only one around who can offer comfort and consolation afterwards? What the children need are other adults who care about them, and to whom they can turn – their own mother, ideally, grandparents and other relatives from both sides of the family (another important reason for keeping access going), friends. It can prevent you and the children becoming too emotionally dependent on each other, which can create enormous difficulties later on. If your teenage daughter has been everything to you for years, she isn't going to take very kindly to any girlfriends you bring home. Equally, you're not going to be at all keen on her boyfriends – even less keen than you would be if the family was still together!

Some fathers do find coping with growing daughters a problem. Many of those interviewed in Tony Hipgrave's study believed they couldn't provide the 'feminine touch' they felt their daughters needed – advice on clothes, information about menstruation and so on.

If you feel you can't cope, then enlist the help of your ex-wife, or if that isn't possible, of a female relative or friend. Your own mother may be willing to help, but her advice and attitudes may be a little out-of-date, so someone younger would be better. If you don't know anyone who can help, then you could approach your daughter's teacher – once you've explained the position, she may well be willing to do what she can.

You might think that this all adds up to a pretty gloomy picture, with nothing but problems, but it would be unrealistic to pretend that bringing up children single-handed, whether you're male or female, is easy.

On the other hand, chances are that, in spite of all the problems, you will make a pretty good job of it.

A divorce court welfare officer who often has to keep an eye on single fathers under a court supervision order, is very impressed with the standard of parenting she comes across.

'I find that men are often much more conscientious than women about bringing up their children, I suppose because they are aware that people are expecting them to make a mess of it. I had one Dad who kept a very careful record of everything he gave his son to eat, to make sure he got enough vitamins and protein and so on. Of course, it wasn't necessary, but it showed how keen he was to do a good job.'

And of course, there are enormous bonuses, too. Many fathers talk about the pride they feel, looking back, in having mastered new skills, and in having coped, and about the pleasure they get from the new, much closer relationship they have with their children.

'I would never have got so close to my two kids as I am now,' said Terry who is in his early thirties. 'I didn't realise until I had to stop work to look after them, that I hardly ever saw my children. I realised then that I'd missed so much those years when I was working, in seeing them grow up.'

Ian, who looked after his children for two years before he remarried, feels the same. 'I think it is unfortunate the way fathers are deprived of close ties with their children because society is organised in such a way that they're out of the house for a minimum of forty hours a week, and so they miss a lot of contact with their children!'

10

Access – Taking the Waiting out of Wanting

All the recent evidence suggests that the children who survive their parents' divorce the best are those who manage to keep up a good relationship with *both* their parents, so it is extremely alarming to learn from several recent surveys, that within two years of divorce, between forty and fifty per cent of the children involved have lost touch completely with the parent who's left home – in the vast majority of cases, the father.

Certainly, where fathers are concerned, problems with access are the source of greatest unhappiness after divorce. In their study of the impact of divorce on men, *Surviving Divorce: Fathers and the Child,* Richard Pennington, John Harper and Peter Ambrose found that almost half the fathers they talked to had lost touch with their children, not because they didn't care or to avoid paying maintenance, but because the whole business was made so distressing and difficult for them and the children that they thought it was best all round if they stayed away. Of the other half who had managed to stay in touch, most had done so in spite of all the problems, not because there weren't any.

'The overwhelming emotions,' said John Harper, 'were of anger and sadness, and they didn't seem to have diminished with time. The sense of failure as a father, and the inability to direct their children's lives came across very strongly indeed.'

Problems with access can seem almost insurmountable.

'When I go to collect my son who's ten, every other Sunday,' said Robin, who's a teacher, 'the front door is opened a few inches and the child is virtually pushed out. I have an access order to see my daughter Jill, too, but it's been over two years since I've seen her. My ex-wife says Jill doesn't want to see me, and while her mother is around, I'm sure that's true. I gather my ex-wife has said to Jill, "Never open the front door, because if you do, a man will come in, put his hand over your face and take you away." It's hardly surprising that my daughter doesn't want to see me.'

Andrew travels 300 miles by train one Sunday a month to see his two children, since their mother decided to move after the divorce. One Sunday, he arrived half an hour late because of a hold-up on the railway, only to have the door slammed in his face by his ex-wife who said, 'If you can't be bothered to get here on time, don't come at all!'

Ken's ex-wife wouldn't let him collect his five-year-old son Simon from the house, so he had to collect the child from outside an underground station. 'I'd return him at five, and when my ex-wife saw us coming, she would start to walk quickly away, so that Simon had to run to catch up with her.'

Jim hasn't seen either of his two children for over five years. Access, which had been difficult for some time, ended after a police sergeant came to see him to investigate allegations that he had 'interfered with' his nine-year-old daughter. 'There wasn't a grain of truth in it, but when I saw my daughter the following weekend, she couldn't look me in the eye. I don't know what had gone on or what had been said to her, but she couldn't look at me even, and it was more than I could bear. The court welfare officer suggested I didn't see kids for a while, but added that my wife had said she wouldn't stop me seeing them in the long-term if I agreed to keep away for six months. Reluctantly, I agreed, and I bitterly regret it now, because in spite of all my efforts I haven't seen my kids since.

'When you lose your husband or wife through divorce, it hurts like hell, but eventually you do get over it. If you lose your children, the scar never heals. I wake up in the morning sometimes, and it's like I lost them yesterday. It breaks your heart.'

Problems with access often reflect the whole dilemma facing divorcing parents in its most acute form – how to separate their feelings about each other and the fact that their marriage is over from their children's needs and their own continuing responsibilities as parents.

Access visits may well be the only remaining link between you and your ex-wife and therefore the only opportunity either of you has for dealing with any 'unfinished business'. If, for instance, you separated suddenly, and all your dealings since have been through lawyers, you won't have had the chance to 'talk your way out of the marriage', to express feelings of anger, hurt or guilt, and to try and make sense of why the marriage failed. Your visits to the children are the only time all those emotions come out.

If the arguments about maintenance, or the house are dragging on, you may find that your ex-wife is creating difficulties about access in order to put pressure on you to give her what she wants.

'I simply had to buy my ex-wife off,' said one father. 'I found that whenever I wanted to see the children it turned out to be "inconvenient". Now that I have given my ex-wife everything from a material point of view, I end up seeing the children whenever I want. But I had to buy that.'

If your ex-wife blames you for the breakdown of the marriage, she may well feel that you don't 'deserve' to see the children, and will make access impossible in order to punish you, failing to realise that she is punishing the children even more, and storing up trouble for herself later on when they turn on her, as they may well do, for depriving them of their father.

In the early stages, after separation, your children might well say that they don't want to see you. Child psychiatrist Robin Benians, whose work brings him into contact with many children of divorced parents, finds this reaction quite common. 'The thinking is, "Daddy's gone away, he's rejected me, I resent that, so I will reject him."' What the parent must do then is keep on trying, stay in touch through phone calls or letters, and constantly reassure the children that he still loves them. You can bet your bottom dollar that in the vast majority of cases, it is only a phase. All children, sooner or later, want to know about the parent who helped make them, not just the parent who looks after them now. And they do feel very anxious about the absent parent – "How is Daddy getting on without me?" – and need to be reassured.'

Even if your children enjoy seeing you, and as far as you can tell, always have a good time on access days, you may find your ex-wife is trying to get access stopped, on the grounds that it upsets them. They become moody or difficult after they've seen you, their school work suffers, or they start bed-wetting, or their asthma gets worse. There are a number of reasons why your children might find access upsetting. As Dr Martin Richards says, 'Children are upset by the fact that their parents have separated, and the time they're most likely to show it is at the time of access. But that is no reason for stopping it. Parents must accept that their children will be upset for a while but it does get less with time, and things do eventually settle down.'

If your children still hanker after the old days when you all lived under the same roof – and the vast majority of children do – then although they enjoy seeing you, it will be painful and upsetting for them to say goodbye. If they can't talk about how they feel when they get home because they're afraid their mother will be angry or will blame you, they will bottle all their emotions up inside, and they will probably come out in other ways – depression, bad behaviour, or inability to concentrate at school.

In their book, *I'm Leaving*, Swedish therapists Bente and Gunnar Oberg tell the story of one boy who was only able to visit his father occasionally and came back from the visits so unhappy that he used to shut himself in his room and cry for a whole day. The mother was so distressed at seeing him suffer so much she began to wonder whether it might not be better to stop the visits, but her new husband was able to make her see that it was her own suffering that she wanted to avoid, and suggested that if the boy saw his father more often the longing and the sadness wouldn't be anything like as acute.

'When the boy returned from the next visit to his father, she was able to welcome him with sympathy, show that she understood how unhappy he was feeling, and eventually, encourage him to talk about it.'

Of course a vital factor in your children's feelings about access will be the attitude of your ex-wife.

If your children are very young, under five or six, they may well believe that you left home because they made you angry, and will be very frightened that, if they make their mother angry, she may leave them too. So, they will do whatever they think she wants them to, and she makes it clear, either in words, or simply by her attitude, that she doesn't want them to see you, they will say they don't want to. Older children are realistic enough to know that their mother isn't going to leave them if they don't go along with her wishes, but they can be made to feel so disloyal in wanting to see you that it is too much to bear. They are also realistic enough to know that they have to live with her the other six days of the week, and if she does make life difficult for them it may be too high a price to pay for a few hours, no matter how much they enjoy them, with you.

'I always say to Mums,' said an experienced divorce court welfare officer, 'that it would be nice if they could tell their children, "Isn't it lovely! You're seeing Dad tomorrow!" instead of "It's access tomorrow. You've got to see *him*!", even if that's what they feel. If Mum is at home sulking when they go, and grumbling about Dad and the state he's let them get into when they get back, they can't tell her they've had a smashing time, and really enjoyed being with Dad, so they say they didn't enjoy it. Then Mum comes along to me, saying she wants access stopped because the kids don't like going!'

A lot of fathers find that where access has been going very smoothly, problems often start when their ex-wife remarries (there can also be problems when you remarry, but those are dealt with in detail in Chapter 12). As Jacqueline Burgoyne and David Clark report in their book *Making a Go of It* (to be published in 1983) which examines second marriages, one of the strongest desires among divorced parents who remarry is to be 'an ordinary family again', which all too often means trying to cut the children off from their other natural parent. Certainly a number of the step-fathers they interviewed felt that their relationship with the children was made more difficult by the fact that their natural father was still around, and were quite happy to take over the financial responsibility for the children if they could stop access.

Dr Robin Benians believes it is an extremely harmful thing to try and do. 'A mother must realise that although it may be awkward or unpleasant for her to see her ex-husband, her children still need to see their real father. If she remarries and gives the children a step-father, she may feel, and the courts unfortunately may agree with her, that the children no longer need any contact with their real father. But it is terribly distressing for a child to be cut off from a parent he cares about – it is such a foolish and unbiological thing to do! A mother must be made to understand that her interests and the children's are *not* the same – he may be her ex-husband, but he will always be their father.'

Some people – fathers included – believe that it is confusing for a child to have a father and a step-father, and therefore it is best for the child if the real father disappears from his/her life. Robin Benians disagrees.

'Even tiny children, who are too young to sort out *why* they have different sets of parents, will be able to appreciate that more than one pair of adults are interested in them. Children in 'ordinary' families are not confused by having a mother, father and two sets of grandparents.

'As far as step-parents go, children are more likely to have a good relationship with their step-parents if they also have good relationships with both their natural parents. If the children have lived with Mum since the break-up, they have got used to having her all to themselves, and will resent having to share her with her new partner. But if they've maintained a good relationship with Dad, that resentment won't be as great.'

Ray found that his access to his son and daughter started to go wrong when his ex-wife married the man for whom she had left him.

'Whenever I went to pick up the children, *he* would bring them out to the car, which was like a red rag to a bull to me, so there were scenes. Then I found my ex-wife had told the kids to call him "Daddy", and it got so bad that the court welfare officer suggested I stopped seeing the children for a year, to give things a chance to settle down.

'As the year was up, the step-father died, and after a bit of a fight, my access to the children was restored. It all went smoothly, until my ex-wife took up with another bloke. Suddenly, they were calling him "Daddy", and the problems started all over again.'

It's not surprising, in the face of problems like these, that many fathers finally reach the conclusion that it might be better all round if they simply disappear from their children's lives.

'It was tearing me apart, seeing him for a few hours once a fortnight and having to hand him back, him in tears saying, "I want to stay with you, Daddy," and usually me in tears too. He was being torn between us and it was really getting to him, so I decided not to carry on. It still hurts like hell, though.'

Dr Robin Benians just can't stress enough how important it is for fathers to stay in touch with their children, no matter how difficult or painful it may be.

'If children no longer see a parent who has been important in their lives, they have to square it off for themselves somehow.

They may think, "Dad can't be bothered with the likes of me because he is so grand and important," and they turn the absent parent into a fantasy ideal figure for themselves, which will interfere with any real relationships they try to make later on in life. Of course no real person, warts and all, can ever live up to a fantasy ideal, so the relationship fails, and they suffer what they see as another rejection.

'It is also very bad for the development of self-esteem. There, the thinking is, "Dad went away because I'm so bad, and doesn't come and see me any more because I'm just not worth it." Some children take that a stage farther and it becomes, "If my Dad doesn't care about me, why should I care about myself? Why should I bother to learn to read? I don't care if I fail. Why should I bother about who those sweets or that money belongs to? I don't care if I get into trouble."

'It's an over simplification to say that divorce causes juvenile delinquency, but we do know, for instance, that children who lose a parent under the age of fourteen are more likely to commit suicide in later life, and that boys with no father in the house are more likely to get into trouble than those from in-tact families.'

A divorce court welfare officer, who in her other role as a probation officer deals with young offenders, supports Dr Benians' view.

'I see a great deal of sadness in the teenagers from broken homes who come into my office. In the course of conversation, I'll ask if they still see their Dad, and they often say, "No, haven't seen him since I was little." I probe a bit and find out what the circumstances were, and sometimes suggest that perhaps Dad stayed away because he felt it would be better for the kids if he did. The answer I get is always the same, though. "No. He can't have thought that much of me, can he, or he'd have stayed in touch. If he'd really loved me, he'd have found a way."

'Whenever Dads are thinking of giving up access because their ex-wives are making it so difficult, I tell them that, and persuade them to keep on trying, no matter how hard it is, even if, for a while, they only write or send postcards. Eventually, when the children are old enough, they can vote with their feet, and obviously it's that much easier to get the relationship going if there's been some contact in the interim.'

Brian was only eight when his parents separated. His mother was very bitter about his father, refused to let Brian see him and told him constantly what a terrible man he was. When he was seventeen, Brian found out where his father was living, and after some hesitation because he wasn't sure what his reception would be like, went and found him. 'He welcomed me into his new family, and in a couple of hours, I felt that the part of me that had been missing all those years, had been put back.'

Other people aren't as lucky as Brian. After years of no contact with their fathers, they've found it impossible to pick up the threads – 'to fill the vacuum', as one man put it – and are left with a sense of mourning for the relationship they never had.

What can you do if you are having problems over access?

If there is a conciliation service in your area, they may be able to help by getting everyone involved – you, your ex-wife, your new partners, and sometimes the children themselves round a table, to try and sort it out. They'll be willing to try and help whether they were involved in working out the arrangements originally, or not (see Chapter 3).

If there isn't a conciliation service near you, then if a divorce court welfare officer was involved in your case, he/she may be willing to mediate, though as Ray found to his cost, he/she may not be as neutral as you might expect.

'It was strictly on the advice of the welfare officer that I agreed, reluctantly, to stop seeing my children for a year when access got difficult. At the end of the year, my ex-wife's husband died, so by the time everything was sorted out, it was almost two years before I was able to get back to court to ask for access to be restored. My ex-wife opposed it, and her key witness was the welfare officer! He said, "I am very doubtful whether it's a good idea for this father to start seeing the children again. We can understand now the step-father has died he is keen to take on the father's role again, but let's not forget that in the year before the step-father died, he showed no interest in his children at all!" I was speechless!'

Ray was able to see his children again, but other fathers who've followed similar advice, have eventually lost all contact with their children because the judge took the view that since access had lapsed, it would be upsetting for the children to start it again. Dr Robin Benians thinks it's a bad idea to suspend access at all. 'It can be extremely harmful to children. The pain produced by separation from parents may cause a child to resist resuming access. It's as if the child is saying, "You abandoned me, and that was so painful that I refuse to see you because I don't want to feel the pain of losing you again."'

If conciliation or mediation isn't successful and you are still having problems seeing your children, then you can go back to court and tell the judge that the access order is not being obeyed. The judge will tell your ex-wife that she must obey the court order, and may even threaten to put her in prison if she doesn't, but if she still flouts the order, there really isn't anything the courts can do.

Technically speaking, they could send her to prison for contempt of court (a number of men are sent to prison each year for disobeying court orders which forbid them to see their children) but in practice they never do because they say it isn't in the interests of the children. They could fine her, but if money is tight, then again, the children are the ones most likely to suffer.

As Sir John Arnold, president of the family division of the High Court has said, where a mother is determined to deny access, the courts are virtually powerless. 'If the iron has entered sufficiently into her soul . . . her attitude to the court will be "Send me to prison if you dare", then usually, we dare not.'

This is at the root of problems over access. The mother who is determined that her ex-husband shall not see the children knows that the courts will let her get away with it. Solicitors, too know that the courts will let mothers get away with it, and advise their clients accordingly.

There have been cases where the mother has deliberately made the whole business of access so difficult and distressing for both the children and the father that the court has decided the only answer was to cancel the access order altogether, even though, as in one case in 1980, the mother's behaviour was 'wholly irrational' and the father's 'blameless'. It's no wonder that fathers feel the odds are heavily stacked against them in the courts.

But there have been signs in the last year or so, that some judges at least are taking a tougher line with mothers who flout access orders.

A London solicitor who has been involved in several such cases recently reports that the judge had warned the mothers involved that if they flouted the orders once more, he would reconsider the whole question of care and control. 'I think if more judges took that attitude, not after the first or second time the case had to go back to court, but when it's happening for the ninth and tenth time, and women realised that they could actually lose their children if they carried on blocking access, the majority would do as they were told. Of course you'd always get some who wouldn't, but they are the exception I'm sure.'

Raymond Gates of Bristol Families Need Fathers heard of another case recently in Wales. 'The father had gone back to court for the umpteenth time because his ex-wife was denying him access to their eight-year-old daughter. The judge made yet another access order, and the mother started saying, "Oh it's no good, it won't work. The child won't do that." The judge looked at her, and said, "You are responsible for the care and control of your child, and if you are telling me that she will not obey you when you tell her she must comply with the order of this court, then perhaps the next time you come before this court I shall be considering a custody order, not an access order." That chap hasn't had a scrap of trouble over access since!'

If you have an order for 'reasonable access' and you are having difficulty in seeing your children, it might be worth asking the court for a defined access order instead. In many ways, defined access orders are not ideal (see Chapter 7) because they don't allow for flexibility, but if the reality of 'reasonable access' is that you don't see your children at all, then three hours between 2pm and 5pm one Sunday a month is better than nothing.

'There was no way of pinning my wife down to "reasonable access",' said Ray, 'so I got a defined access order for two hours a month. What it meant was I had a definite starting point from which I could negotiate. Once I started seeing the kids again, they began to complain that two hours wasn't enough, so we took it from there.'

Don found a defined access order the solution to his problems, too. 'When it was "reasonable access", my ex-wife used to put terrible pressure on my daughter by saying, "You don't have to go unless you *really* want to," and making her feel terribly disloyal if she said she did. With the defined order, my daughter could say she *had* to come and see me on alternate Sundays whether she wanted to or not, which took the pressure off her.'

Making access work

Perhaps the hardest thing you have to adjust to is the change in your relationship with your children. Instead of seeing them every day, even if it is only briefly over breakfast or for a goodnight kiss before they go to sleep, you'll see them once a week if you're lucky, and then only for a few hours.

Many fathers feel, after divorce, that they don't have a real role to play in their children's lives any more, that because they can no longer help, support and guide their children on a day-to-day basis, they weren't proper parents any longer and therefore didn't matter.

But children don't see it that way – they need *both* their parents and the fact that you are still around, loving them, taking an interest in them, matters more than the fact that you're not there to help with homework, or for a quick game of snakes and ladders before bed.

Obviously how you treat access is very important. Though it is difficult for many reasons, you should try and keep the relationship as *natural* as possible. So that, as Dr Martin Richards puts is, 'access isn't a visit, it's a sharing of everyday life.'

With good will on all sides, it can be done. When Keith and his wife Liz decided to separate three years ago, when he fell in love with someone else, they were both determined that their three children should suffer as little disruption as possible.

'We couldn't bear the idea of them being put on a timetable, which is what the solicitors wanted us to do. Mine said, "If you don't, you won't see them at all after a while. Whenever you want to pick them up, there'll be problems." But we resisted it, and decided that the children should have access to us, not the other way round.

'Liz stayed in the family home, which was familiar territory for the kids, and I took a flat on their way home from school, big enough to sleep me and the three of them.

'They're thirteen, twelve and ten now, and they've each got a key. Sometimes, I get home from work and one, two or all of them will be there. Sometimes they'll stay five minutes then go home, other times they'll stay for supper then decide it's not worth going home, so they'll ring Liz and say they're staying with me.

'A couple of months back, the little lad said he wanted to come and live with me, which is what he's done. When I'm working late, or away for the night, he'll go round to the "girls" for supper or for the night. Some people might say that an arrangement like ours is confusing for the kids, but I must say they show no signs of confusion whatsoever!'

In her research on access, Sheila Burns found the children who were most content about their parents' divorce were those with flexible access arrangements, who had had some say in working them out.

Obviously, this kind of flexible access can only work if you and your ex-wife are prepared to put your children first, and not let your feelings about each other dictate the way you behave. If you can make it work though, everyone benefits.

Your ex-wife benefits because having total responsibility for the children all the time is very wearing, and it makes it extremely difficult for her to rebuild a life of her own.

'I always talk about access in those terms to my women clients,' said a woman solicitor. 'I say, "Wouldn't it be nice if you had every other weekend to yourself?", and the answer is almost always "yes", whereas if I put the other way – "Would you like your husband to have the kids every other weekend?" – then I'm sure the answer in some cases, anyway, would have been "no"!'

The children benefit because you still play a significant, natural part in their lives. You're not the man they don't really know who turns up once a month and takes them round the museum or to the park yet again for a couple of hours, before disappearing again. And you benefit, of course, because you still feel you do matter to your children.

But in the majority of cases, sadly, it doesn't work like that. Your ex-wife may insist that your access is within clearly defined limits, and may even invoke the law if you overstep them.

Bob took his three children for a week's holiday last summer, and they were all having such a marvellous time that he contacted his ex-wife through a friend (they weren't speaking) and asked if they could stay an extra day. 'The message came back "No", so the kids rang and begged her to let them stay, but she wouldn't change her mind even though it wouldn't have interfered with her plans at all.

'We talked about it, the kids and I and decided we'd stay on anyway, and sent her a message to that effect. Seven o'clock that evening, there was a knock on the door. It was a policeman who said that there was a court order for the kids to be back home that afternoon. In fact there was no court order – there was just a letter from her solicitor to mine – but it shows how far she was prepared to go to stop us.'

If your ex-wife decides to move, or even emigrate (see Chapter 7), it can make access extremely difficult, if not impossible. Even if you can afford to travel 300 miles every weekend to see the children for a few hours, like before, what are you going to do with them? Outside big towns, there is little to do on a Sunday, and even if there is, the safari park or the museum palls on the fourth or fifth visit.

In that situation, it might be better to try and arrange to have the children to stay for a weekend once a month, say, assuming you've got room. Don't worry too much if your new home is a bit bleak or a bit scruffy compared to the old family home. Your children want to see where you live, so they can picture you in your new setting. They'll also want to feel that they belong there, too, so create a space for them, even if it's only a corner, where they can stick up pictures and photos or keep their toys, so that when they do come and see you, they don't feel like visitors.

If you simply don't have the room to put them up, then perhaps you could arrange to stay with relations or, if you're on sufficiently good terms with your ex-wife, to stay in the family home while she has a weekend away.

If you have no-one who could help, then contact the Families Need Fathers group either where you're living or where your ex-wife and the children are living. In some areas, members will offer accommodation to fathers and children who can't see each other any other way. If you are able to see your children only once a fortnight or once a month, it is very tempting to try and cram all the affection you've been unable to give them into those few hours and spoil them with presents and treats – in other words, to be not so much a father as a Father Christmas.

The best solution is to spend more time together, so the relationship can be a more normal one, but if that just isn't possible, then resist the urge to spoil them. For one thing, your children will start to think of you only in terms of what they can get out of you, and if your ex-wife can't afford to do the same, she may well resent you trying to 'buy' the children's affection, which is how she'll see it.

Same with behaviour. If you let the children run riot while they're with you, because understandably you don't want to spend what little time you have together ticking them off, then don't be surprised if your ex-wife, who has to deal with over-excited, rude children who keep saying, 'But Dad lets us . . . ,' isn't enthusiastic about access. Children are very quick to exploit any disagreements, and to play one off against the other, so it will make life easier if you can agree a basic set of rules with your ex-wife – bedtime, and just how much coco cola can be drunk in the course of a day.

Dr Martin Richards doesn't think that's essential though. 'It is simply enough to make it clear to them that rules between homes may differ, and the fact that they are allowed to do X in the other home is no reason why they should do it here. Far from seeing differences in rules and routines in two homes as confusing for children, I think there are good reasons for seeing them as an advantage. They are ways of seeing something of variety in life, and learning that there is not always a single answer to a problem.'

On your side, it is extremely important that you are totally reliable about access. If you say you will be there at ten on Saturday, then be there at ten and if there is a very good reason why you can't make it, ring and let the children know. There are few things that upset children more than getting excited about a promised visit, waiting anxiously by the door, only to be disappointed. It's the kind of behaviour that will make your ex-wife angry – she'll have to deal with unhappy, let-down children after all – and make her want to stop access altogether.

'What I suggest Dads do,' said a divorce court welfare officer, 'is buy the kids a calendar, and sit down with them to mark in red all the days they'll be seeing each other. Kids like that because it's up there on their wall and they know when they'll be seeing Dad again without having to pester Mum all the time.'

Although it may be tempting to use the children as messengers or spies, don't! If you and your ex-wife are arguing about maintenance, then talk direct or, if you must, through your solicitors, but don't involve the children. Don't quiz them about your ex-wife's private life or force them into a position where they have to keep secrets about yours.

'I was chatting to my daughter about an outing she'd been on with her mother,' said Tony, 'and in the course of conversation, she mentioned "Doug". I asked, "Who's Doug?", and she said, "Oh, Mummy's boyfriend," then clapped her hand over her mouth and said and looked horrified. "Mummy said I wasn't to tell you about that!" she said and was so upset that it took me ages to reassure her that I wouldn't let on.'

However bitter you may feel about your ex-wife, don't criticise her to the children. They love both of you, and it hurts them to be told that someone they love is no good. Don't try and divide their loyalties more than they are already divided – don't ask which of you they love most or where they really want to live.

Above all, be *flexible* and remember that access is much their right – if not more so – as it is yours. If you insist that they come to you every single Sunday because that's what the court order says, even when it means missing their best friend's birthday party, or a trip to the circus, don't be surprised if you have sulky, rebellious children on your hands, who come to think of access as rather like having to go to church. Include their friends in outings sometimes – you would if you were still living at home.

Remember that as they grow up, their needs will change and you must be prepared to change access arrangements to meet those needs.

When they're very small toddlers, 'little and often' is probably the best rule. They have no sense of time, and it's meaningless to tell them you'll see them in a week because to them, that is eternity. Equally, it's probably not a good idea to take them away for a weekend, say, because at that age they will fret for their mother, as they would for whoever is bringing them up.

Once they reach five or six, they can understand time, and can cope with knowing they'll see you in a week. They'll also be happy to spend a weekend or even a week's holiday with you without fretting for their mother.

Once they reach their pre-teens and teens, they'll develop full lives of their own, so don't be hurt if they don't want to see you so often. You wouldn't see that much of them even if you were still living at home. They still need you, but in a different way.

Making access work can be extremely hard work, but it is worth persevering. We know the damage a 'broken home' can inflict on children, but that needn't always be the inevitable result of divorce. As Keith put it, 'As far as our kids are concerned, family life hasn't broken down. It's just that Mum and Dad live in different houses.'

11

The Emotional Impact of Divorce

Many people, going through divorce, find that they are simply not prepared at all for the emotional and physical effects the experience has on them.

If your marriage has been unhappy for sometime, and the decision to end it has only come after a lot of painful heart-searching, you might expect to feel a sense of relief that the uncertainty is now over. Instead, you find that you are experiencing a whole range of painful and sometimes conflicting emotions.

If you have left home for someone else, there will be guilt feelings to contend with. If you have children, who are obviously deeply upset by your decision to leave, then the guilt may be almost unbearable. You almost certainly don't hate your wife – in fact although your feelings have changed, you probably still care about her a lot – and the pain you know you are causing her only makes the guilt worse. You may find you are taking it out on your new partner, blaming her, unjustly, for breaking up your marriage, or putting her under enormous pressure to make your relationship so perfect that you feel justified in leaving home and creating so much unhappiness. It's not surprising that the relationships for which people leave home often don't last.

You may find it impossible to talk about your feelings because, after all, 'it's all your own fault', and you know that you could probably go back home if you wanted to.

Guilt may turn into anger and aggression. You're the one who's causing all the pain, but you find it so unbearable that the only way of coping with it is to blame your wife for what has happened. Gary, who was divorced four years ago, was on the receiving end. 'One night after we'd both been drinking, we had a terrible row in which she said it was all my fault she was going off with this other bloke. If I hadn't been so boring and gutless, she would never have gone and left me. At the time, I thought, "Of course she's right. It is all my fault," but now I realise why she said it. She was never any good at handling guilt.'

If you're the one who's been left, you will probably feel angry and aggressive, too, blaming your wife for wrecking your marriage and refusing to see that you have any responsibility for it at all. In their book *I'm Leaving* Swedish therapists Bente and Gunnar Oberg stress how important it is for divorcing couples to be able to express their anger to each other. 'Confrontation is the only means of emotional release and preventing aggression from becoming destructive. It is most unfortunate that so many people going through divorce conduct the struggle by proxy – the lawyer's role is to attack the other party and defend his own client – thus causing the partners to remain fixed in their aggression and bitterness.'

Whether you are the one who wants the divorce or not, you may feel an enormous sense of failure. Marriage after all is presented as the most normal framework for a relationship, something that most people seem to manage, and yet you've made a hash of it.

If your wife has left you for someone else, or has simply decided that she doesn't want to live with you any more, which many people find even harder to bear, then the sense of rejection can be overwhelming, and your self-confidence can be totally shattered.

As one man put it, 'The person who mattered most to me had said I wasn't good enough, and since she knew me better than anyone else in the world, she had to be right.'

It's not surprising that the emotional turmoil caused by separation and divorce can be so great that it manifests itself as physical illness.

In their research on the effects of divorce on men, Peter Ambrose, John Harper and Richard Pennington found that the impact on health was 'massive'. The majority of the men they interviewed reported sleeplessness, headaches, anxiety, weight-loss, and many stress-related illnesses – problems with their hearts, stomachs, bowels and so on.

'Men are brought up not to be very emotional,' said John Harper, 'and therefore their resources for dealing with emotional crises are very limited. Although they need help just as much as women do, they don't seek it as readily. Something like ninety per cent of women seek help from their doctor after separation or divorce, but less than half the men in our survey had done so.'

You may find that your own doctor is very helpful, and understands your need to talk about the emotional problems underlying the physical symptoms about which you've gone to see him or her. But many family doctors simply don't have the time to spend with you, and will simply prescribe tranquillisers, sleeping tablets or something to help with your indigestion.

If you're a member of a church, you might find that the vicar or minister will be willing to talk about the problems with you, or perhaps refer you to a pastoral service. But if that isn't an option, who can you talk to?'

Relations may be willing to listen, but they may not be able to offer the sympathetic, but objective ear that you need. Being told, 'I never did like her!' or, 'You're better off out of that! Plenty more pebbles on the beach!' isn't actually going to help.

You could talk to friends, of course, but if they are also friends of your wife, you may be reluctant to say what you really feel, and they may be unwilling to be seen to be taking sides. And there is a limit to the number of evenings you can spend in their living room pouring your heart out till the small hours. Even the closest friends get bored with it after a while, and they become reluctant to invite you over on social occasions in case you start recounting in detail the contents of the latest letter from your wife's solicitors, or going on about what a grasping bitch she's become!

It could well be that your friends will be more valuable to you *after* the crisis is over, and you are picking up the threads of your life again, so perhaps you'd be better off talking through your problems with a detached outsider, someone who knows what you're going through and who can help you come to terms with what's happened, and put it in perspective.

There are a number of places you can go for counselling and help. In spite of their name, and their image, Marriage Guidance is willing to help you at *any* stage of the divorce process with any emotional problems you may have, (see page 13).

The Trust of the National Council for the Divorced and Separated has set up a number of divorce counselling services around the country (see page 151 for a full list), staffed by volunteers, often people who have been divorced themselves, who are specially trained by the Trust. Their approach is short-term, rather than long-term, and they will try and help by 'looking at all the problems facing you, practical and emotional, at one go, helping you to see a way through them so that you can pick up the threads of your life again.' The service is free, and in fact, donations are actively discouraged, because, according to Muriel Stanley of the National Council for the Divorced and Separated, if people knew that they were expected to contribute, those who couldn't afford very much, wouldn't use the service.

If you live or work in the London area, you could try the Divorce and Conciliation Advisory Service in Victoria (see page 151), whose trained staff can offer advice on all aspects of divorce, and support while you're going through it. They will conciliate between you and your wife if you want them to, or they will see you alone. At the time of writing they charge £15 for the first visit and £10 an hour for subsequent visits, though if you really can't afford the fees, they will reduce them or waive the charge altogether.

In some towns and cities, like Leicester, Stoke, Edinburgh, and some London boroughs, there are now divorce experience courses, and although they vary slightly from place to place, the main aim is the same – to help people who are thinking about divorce, or who are going through it to understand the realities – practical, social and emotional. In Leicester, for example, the courses are run on three consecutive Monday evenings, and consist of group sessions, led by a divorce court welfare officer, in which people share their experiences. Like many people, you may find it very reassuring just to know that what you're feeling is not unique, and that lots of other people have the same reactions. If there is so much anger between you and your wife that you can't even begin to see each other's point of view, you may find it very valuable to hear someone else's wife expressing her feelings and describing what divorce is doing to her.

Your initial reaction might well be that admitting you need help is a sign of weakness, and that thousands of other people cope without counselling or courses, so why can't you?

Some people do cope very well, it's true, but an awful lot of people don't. Some have taken much longer to get over the experience than they would have done with just a little help, and others haven't got over it all. That's not to say that counselling can remove all pain from divorce – nothing can do that – but it can stop the experience from being more painful than it need be, and help you get back to normal. A good analogy is breaking a bone. If you do nothing, it may knit together in time, but it will be extremely painful, and it will never be straight again. If you have it set by a doctor, it will still take time to mend, and it will still hurt for a while, but once it has healed, it will be almost as good as new.

If your divorce is a long-drawn-out, bitterly contested affair, you may find that during the separation, all your energies are engaged in the battles over the house or the children, and you begin to look forward to the day your decree absolute is granted as the day when all your problems will be over.

Of course, it isn't always like that. Many people have been shaken to find that instead of a great flood of relief, and excitement about a fresh start, they feel an almost overwhelming sense of sadness and of loss. In a way, it isn't surprising. When you got married, presumably you loved your wife and had great hopes for your future together, and so when it all goes wrong, you mourn for those lost hopes, for the good times, and for the years you feel you wasted. These feelings will probably start to fade quite quickly as you start your new life, but it's important to recognise them, and not try to pretend they don't exist.

If you haven't embarked on a new relationship right away then you may well find, as one counsellor put it that 'the flip-side of freedom is loneliness!'

The end of your marriage means that you have not only lost your wife, but your children, your home and the whole framework of your life, and if you lived at home before you married, you'll be living on your own for the first time in your life. Chances are that you won't have been able to set yourself up in a comfortable new home right away, and even if you have, the prospect of going home to an empty house every evening after work isn't very appealing, so your social life becomes more important than before. But it will have changed. Some of your friends will have sided with your ex-wife, others, determined not to get involved, will have drifted away, and some of those you keep may well see you in a different light. Society is still geared to couples, and though it is still easier for a single man than it is for a single woman, it can present problems.

You may still be welcomed by the woman of the house, to make up the numbers or even as someone for her to flirt with, but her husband may see you as a threat, even though any kind of emotional or sexual entanglement is the last thing on your mind.

It's somehow assumed that when a man is divorced, his male friends all rally round, but John Harper and his colleagues didn't find that to be the case, and a number of men in their survey had lost friends as a result of their divorce. 'There's a feeling somehow that those who get divorced are rocking the boat, that it's all right to fool around, but not to get caught because that puts the pressure on everyone else, or that it might start giving their own wives ideas. It's hard to pinpoint exactly what form it takes, but there is still a stigma attached to divorce.'

You might feel that old friends are part of your former life, and seeing them brings back too many memories, so it might be better to try and make some new friends, or you may move, and so have no choice, but where do you start?

Most towns these days have a club for the divorced and separated, either run to commercial lines, like the Solo clubs or on a voluntary basis, like those organised by the National Council for the Divorced and Separated (see page 151 for addresses).

Some people have found them very valuable.

'It was marvellous to be with people I didn't have explain anything to,' said Paul who's in his late thirties, 'because they'd all been through it, so they knew!

'It took me a while to get round to going, partly because I'd been told these places were full of women looking for husbands, but if there were any there, they didn't cross my path. What I did find were lots of women who weren't ready for another serious relationship yet, and who just wanted a bit of fun and companionship, like I did!'

Steve, who's in his early fifties, wasn't so lucky. 'I went along to one of these clubs in York, and I stayed about ten minutes. There was such a feeling of failure and despair that I walked out, saying to myself, "You can sustain more life on your own than you could with that lot!"'

Of course, clubs vary, and it might be worth two or three, if you can, before you abandon the idea altogether. If it takes a lot of courage to go along in the first place, because your self-confidence is still badly dented, and it doesn't work out first time, don't assume it's all your fault. It's just that it wasn't the right club for you. If there aren't any special clubs in your area, then think about joining an ordinary club, or an adult education class. It's the sort of advice that agony aunts dish out all the time, but there is a lot of sense in it. It means that you'll be meeting people with whom you already have something in common, and if you find it very hard to break the ice, then going along to the badminton club or a cookery class means that you can concentrate on your drop shots or your drop scones until you're ready to take the plunge. Do join the sort of class that gives you a chance to chat – cookery or upholstery for instance – rather than one which involves sitting still and listening to the teacher for a couple of hours.

There will come a time, sooner or later, when you feel ready for another relationship with a woman. A popular image of the divorced man is Bachelor Days Revisited, with strings of girlfriends always available, but for most men, it isn't like that at all.

'When I first took a woman out after my divorce,' said Alan, 'I felt as gauche and shy as a sixteen-year-old. Having been married for eighteen years, I'd forgotten about courting and how painful a lot of it was – wondering whether I was talking too much or boring her, wondering whether she'd think I was trying to get her drunk if I persuaded her to have a brandy, and then when I drove her home, whether she was expecting me to kiss her, and if she asked me in for coffee, whether it meant coffee and if it didn't, what I wanted to do about it . . . I didn't relax for a moment, the whole evening. Some men enjoy all that, the thrill of the chase and so on, but not me!'

If your children live with you, then obviously starting a new relationship is much more complicated. First you have to decide whether to introduce them to your girlfriends or not. It could be very unsettling for them to meet a whole string of 'aunties', so you might decide that you'll only introduce them to someone you're serious about. But then, if you can't afford babysitters a couple of nights a week, how are you going to get to the stage where you know whether you're serious about her without bringing her home, and introducing her to the children? If they've got used to having you all to themselves, they may not take kindly to any 'intruder'. As Dr Robin Benians says, 'From the time children begin to talk until they are old enough to have a sex life of their own and understand your needs a bit more, they are going to give hell to anyone who comes along, and do their damnedest to see them off!'

And what about your sex life – what do you do if you want to sleep together? Do you tell the children honestly, and risk their disapproval – children and adolescents can be very moralistic! – or should you go through a routine of phony door slamming and loud 'Goodnights', before you creep up the stairs together, and run the risk of your six-year-old finding 'Auntie' in your bed when he stumbles in, unable to sleep, in the small hours?

There are no easy answers. Some men find that more or less total celebacy for a while is the answer – having gone through an initial burst of frantic sexual activity, they find casual affairs very unsatisfactory anyway, so it isn't really very difficult to stop, while others manage to have relationships without it upsetting the children. Certainly, if you have a good relationship with your ex-wife and the children see her often, then life is less difficult. For one thing, it will give you the time and the privacy you need, and for another, your children are less likely to feel threatened by someone new coming into your life.

If your children don't live with you, then obviously it is much easier to start a new relationship, because you have plenty of time without the children around to get to know each other.

At the beginning, it's only natural that you'll want to spend as much time as you can with her, and since you think she's terrific, you might convince yourself that your children will, too, and so invite her along when you see them.

Be warned! It is very unlikely that your children will feel the same way about her, no matter how terrific she is. After all, they only see you once a week or once a fortnight, and so they're not going to be very happy about sharing you with someone else, especially if you seem much more interested in her than you are in them!

It's a good idea to introduce them to her gradually, drop her name into the conversation once or twice, but don't give her such a big build-up that the children are expecting Princess Diana or Mary Poppins because when they finally do meet her, they will inevitably be disappointed. Make the first meeting fairly brief. If you have them all day, then perhaps she could pop in for tea. Next time, perhaps you could go out for the afternoon together, but make sure you always spend some of the time alone with them. That way, they won't feel they're being supplanted in your affections, and it will give them a chance to get to know her gradually so that a natural relationship can develop. Remember, you can't make them like her, much as you want to, and the more you try, the less likely they are to accept her.

The resentment, if there is any, may not all be on one side. Your girlfriend may resent the time you spend with your children, or feel jealous of the contact you have with your ex-wife as a result, especially if you are on good terms.

It is very important for you to rebuild a life for yourself, but on the other hand, you must make it clear, right from the start, that your children are very important to you, so that she is in no doubt that she is taking on a father with responsibilities, not a man with no commitments.

'If I've made a date, and the kids ring up and say they're coming round,' said Keith, 'then I rearrange the date for another evening, because I've said that the kids shall have access to me whenever they want, and I mean it. If the woman doesn't understand, then the relationship had no future, anyway.'

It's no good avoiding the issue early on, and telling yourself that you'll cope with it later on, because 'later on' always comes and it will be much more difficult and painful to resolve.

You may also find when you start a new relationship that your ex-wife begins making life difficult over the children. She may try and stop them seeing you altogether, or insist that 'she' isn't around when you do. Technically speaking, you can spend your time with the children how, and with whom, you like, unless the court has ordered otherwise. But as we've already seen, if your ex-wife wants to make access difficult, or impossible, it is very easy for her to do so, so it might be worth biding your time and waiting till she gets used to the idea before you involve your girlfriend. If the problems are dragging on, it's worth trying conciliation – they are used to involving new partners in sorting out problems – or as a last resort, you can go back to court, but that's not likely to solve the problem, and may create even more bitterness.

12

'The Triumph of Hope over Experience' Marrying Again

All the statistics show that the majority of people who divorce, marry again, and surprisingly quickly. Over a third of marriages today involve one partner who has been married before, and in one-ninth of marriages, both partners have been married before. In 1977, a third of those who remarried did so within three months of their divorce, and of all those who remarried within a five year period, sixty per cent had done so within a year of their divorce.

In some cases, of course, people only get divorced in order to marry again, so it isn't surprising that they remarry very quickly. But even people who don't meet their new partner until after the breakdown of their first marriage seem to marry with some speed, men even more quickly than women.

You might think that, having had their fingers burnt once, divorced men would be very reluctant to get involved again. But then, as we've seen life after divorce can leave a lot to be desired. For many men, who don't live with their children, loneliness can be acute. They miss family life, and the chance to start a second family, or to inherit a ready-made one can seem very appealing. On a more practical level, men who've had to leave the family home and are paying maintenance are often forced to live in pretty miserable rented accommodation, or even to move back in with their parents, and their only chance of establishing a comfortable, or independent life for themselves again is to move in with a woman with a home of her own, or to take out a mortgage on the strength of two incomes.

If you are thinking of marrying again, you should ask yourself a number of questions. Are you marrying again simply because you are lonely, or because you want to be half of a couple again? Or is it just because you have had enough of roughing it and want a few home comforts? Or do you want to prove that *somebody* wants you, even if your ex-wife didn't, and therefore, you're not the one who can't make relationships work?

None of these are good reasons for embarking on a second marriage – at least, not if you're hoping that the marriage will last!

You should also ask yourself whether you have really come to terms with the failure of your first marriage. Renate Olins of the London Marriage Guidance Council believes that the success of a second marriage depends to a large extent on the way your first marriage ended. 'If you emerge from your first marriage thinking, "I gave her everything a woman could want, and this is how she repays me!", then your chances of making your second marriage work are not too good. Anyone embarking on a second marriage should be determined to avoid the mistakes that ended the first, and before you can avoid them, you must be able to recognise what they were!'

The evidence suggests that many people who remarry *are* aware of the mistakes they made first time round, and make a conscious effort to avoid repeating them. They also approach a second marriage with more realistic expectations, and in a more calculated way, having weighed up all the pros and cons, or so Jacqueline Burgoyne found in her four-year study of second marriages in Sheffield.

'Couples in our study tended to speak of increasing closeness, shared interests, a gradual awareness that they wanted to get married. They don't tend to talk, as couples marrying for the first time tend to talk, about "falling in love" or eyes meeting across a crowded room, and all that.'

But in spite of that, and in spite of people's determination to 'make a go of it' second time round, second marriages are now even more likely to break down than first marriages – over forty per cent now end in divorce. So what goes wrong?

You might find it very hard to accept that your wife has been married before, especially if you move into her old family home. You may be jealous of the past, and if her ex-husband was the one who wanted the divorce, you may feel you are very much second choice. As one man put it, 'If he hadn't left her for this other woman, they'd still be married and Anna would never even have dreamt of marrying me. It's absurd, I know, but I live in dread of his second marriage breaking down because at the back of my mind, there is always the thought that if he wanted Anna back, he could probably have her.'

You might find, like many men do, that your previous marriage is a continuing source of aggravation in your life. If your ex-wife wants to be vindictive and is continually asking for more maintenance, or keeps chopping and changing the arrangements for the children (one father found after he remarried that his ex-wife 'couldn't cope with the children any longer' every time he and his second wife planned to go away) it can place an intolerable strain on your second marriage especially if your second wife feels she is working to support the first, and can't afford to stop and have a family of her own.

If you have children, then there are a number of points to consider before you marry again. If your children live with you, and you are thinking about remarrying mainly to give them a mother, then think again. A lot of recent evidence suggests that it is more stressful for children to live through their parents' remarriage than it is to go on living in a single-parent family. For one thing, your remarriage is likely to reduce the amount of contact they have with their real mother, which will be very distressing for them. For another having got used to having you all to themselves, they will almost certainly resent the fact that a lot of your energies and emotions are being directed towards your new wife.

If you are seriously thinking of marrying again, you can't ask your children's permission, exactly, but you must discuss it with them, and find out how they feel. If they seem strongly opposed to the idea, or really can't stand their prospective step-mother, then you have a problem. It's not something you can ignore in the hope that it will go away – it won't – and if you take the view that if you are happy, then eventually they will be too, you are in for a nasty shock.

The question you then have to ask yourself is which is more important the children's happiness or your own? If you go ahead and marry her anyway, then the children will do their damnedest to destroy the relationship, and make everyone miserable in the process. And on top of that, if you feel that you are sacrificing the children's happiness to your own, the guilt may be overwhelming.

If you don't marry her, you may resent the children for the 'sacrifice' they have 'forced' you to make, and feel that they must compensate you somehow for what you've given up.

It isn't an easy choice, but in Tony Hipgrave's study of lone fathers, all the men who had been faced with the problem had put their children first. 'You've only got them a few years,' one father said, and Pat, whose girlfriend moved out after clashes over his son, said, 'Even now she says to me I give my kids too much love, I put them before her, which to me is wrong. You *should* put your kids first anyway. I mean, kids can't bring themselves up.'

Even if the children seem to like your girlfriend, there may be problems when you actually marry. From the children's point of view, there is a huge difference between having someone around sometimes who is usually very nice to them, and having someone living in all the time who moans about mud on the carpet, or who nags them about their homework.

Even if your new wife is the soul of tact, and leaves all the discipline to you, the children may still react badly to the fact that you are now actually married.

According to Dr Robin Benians, it isn't uncommon. 'Many children after divorce still hanker after the "good old days" when Mum and Dad lived together under the same roof, and no matter how bad things may seem, until another marriage actually takes place, the way back is still open. Mum or Dad marrying again finally puts an end to this hope.'

On the other hand, as long as the children think there is a possibility of you and your ex-wife getting back together – in other words, while you and your girlfriend still aren't married – they may go on behaving badly in an attempt to drive the 'intruder' away. Once the deed is done, they may well accept the situation. Again, if they have a good relationship with their mother, and don't feel that your new wife is trying to take her place, they may well accept her more readily.

If there are problems between your children and your second wife, then the most difficult situation you will find yourself in is being caught in the cross-fire between them, especially since they will both feel they are entitled to your undivided loyalty. You may well feel guilty about your children – after all, they didn't want you to get divorced, and they certainly didn't choose their step-mother – and so you may be tempted to side with them, but once they realise they can create trouble between you, they will not be slow to exploit it. Equally, your second wife will resent your taking the children's side against her, and it isn't going to make her feel any more kindly disposed towards them.

So whose side do you take?

'If you want the marriage to work,' said Renate Olins, 'there is only one answer to that question. You side with your partner. Your children, much as you love them, will grow up and move away. If you have married again, then presumably your partner is the person with whom you want to spend the rest of your life.'

Certainly it's not going to do any of you any good if the second marriage ends in divorce. The fact that you and your children have been through it before doesn't make it any easier or any less painful the second time around.

It's more likely, though, that your children will live with their mother, and only see you at weekends, and in the holidays, and though many of the same problems can arise, the pressure is nothing like as great simply because they aren't with you all the time.

But if your second wife has children, chances are they will be living with you, which can create difficulties with your own children, especially if you don't see them quite as often as before, and they may be extremely hostile to their step-brothers and sisters.

Obviously, it is very easy to see your step-children as substitutes for your own, with whom you gradually lose touch, and to try and cut their real father out of their lives. But remember, no matter how fond you are of them, they are *not* your children. They have a father of their own whom they still need to see, in the same way that your own children still need to see you.

As Jacqueline Burgoyne and her colleague David Clark discovered, a lot of step-families feel the need to try and 'pass' as ordinary, unbroken families, and pretend that the children's other, real parent (and all their other relations on that side of the family) don't exist, which can create all kinds of problems (see page 120). But others accept that they are a different kind of family, an extended family, and make the most of what it offers – relationships with lots of adults, not just real and step-parents, but sets of real and step-relatives, too.

On a day-to-day basis, coping with 'yours' and 'mine' demands the wisdom of Solomon – or at least the ability to be scrupulously fair. You almost certainly won't feel the same spontaneous love for your step-children as you feel for your own, and may therefore bend over backwards to be nice to them, so that your own children lose out. You can't make yourself feel the same way about your own, and your step-children (if you're honest, you don't feel the same about each of your own children!) but if you're aware of your feelings, then at least you can treat them all the same.

You may find other relatives aren't as sensitive as you are – grandparents, for example, who arrive laden with presents for their natural grandchildren, but with nothing for the 'steps'. It's worth having a discreet word, explaining the friction that it causes, and asking them to bring less expensive presents for all the children, or to bring nothing at all.

Before you marry and take on someone else's children, you should consider very carefully what it means. Do you think their mother is too soft with them and that they're out of control? Do you really like them, and just as important, do they like you, and what can you do about it if they don't?

When John moved in with Pat and her two daughters, who were eleven and nine, he didn't know what had hit him. 'The first year was hell! I had eggs thrown at me, fruit, anything that was handy – in fact, during that time, we had to buy a new television, and I bought one with doors, just so the screen wouldn't get smashed! They tore my clothes, hid my razor, and wouldn't speak to me. If anyone had told me that two little girls could make me so unhappy for so long, I would never have believed it.

'It got so bad that I even thought of leaving Pat – not because I didn't love her, but because the girls were really getting to me. In the end, we decided to give it six months to see if we couldn't fetch them round. Luckily, in the end, we did.'

It is extremely hurtful if your step-children are hostile and make no secret of how they feel. The fact that you are an adult and meant to be above such things doesn't help one bit.

Dr Robin Benians feels it is best to be honest with the children about how you feel. 'You could say to them, "I'm here because I love your Mum, and that doesn't mean I have to love *you*, but since we do have to live together, let's try and learn to get on!" Children are often so flattered that adults bother to be honest with them that it could mean the start of a better relationship.'

Since children are quick to exploit differences between you, decide at the very start who is going to be responsible for discipline, and what the basic rules are going to be. There are few things more likely to cause a marriage to run into difficulties than you or your wife shouting at each other, 'How dare you treat my children like that!' Finally, don't make things even harder for yourself by thinking that you ought to love your step-children, and feeling horribly guilty if you can't. It would be like saying that you *ought* to love your in-laws, and nobody would expect that! If you treat your step-children as individuals, and give yourselves time to get to know each other, so that a relationship can grow naturally between you, then it can work very well.

One of the major factors in your children's response to your marrying again, of course, is the kind of relationship you have had with them since the divorce.

Keith's children call in and see him most days on their way home from school, and though initially, they were very wary about him marrying again, in the last year, they've actually started trying to marry him off. 'They say things like "Sarah's mum's divorced. She's ever so nice. You'd like her. I'm sure she'd like to go out with you. Shall I ask her for you?" It's not that they want a new mum – after all they've got a mum that they live with – it's more that now they're in their teens they're beginning to realise that a sexual and emotional life is very important, and I think they worry about my being lonely when they're not around.'

Appendix

Scotland and Northern Ireland

Although the divorce laws in Scotland are now broadly similar to those in England and Wales, there are still some differences. Some of the terminology is different – the petitioner is 'the pursuer' and the respondant, 'the defender' and the petition itself is 'the summons'.

As for the 'kiss-and-make-up' provision, if you are petitioning on the grounds of adultery, unreasonable behaviour or desertion, you are allowed a three-month period to try and sort out your differences which starts on the day you start living together again, and ends exactly three months later, regardless of how long you have actually lived together in that time. If you are divorcing on the grounds of two or five years separation, then you are allowed a six-month period. If you live together after the period allowed has expired, you are deemed to have forgiven your wife and you can't divorce her on those grounds.

All divorces in Scotland are heard in the Court of Session in Edinburgh (the equivalent of the High Court), not in the sheriff courts (which combine the fuctions of magistrates courts and county courts in England and Wales), although they can deal with some matrimonial matters. The process of getting a divorce begins in much the same way as it does in England and Wales (see page 57), with your seeing a solicitor and giving him details of your marriage and why it has broken down. After that, it does become more complicated than in England. Since January 1983, it's been possible to get a 'postal' divorce but only if the divorce is undefended, if the grounds are two years' separation with consent or five years separation without consent, if there are no children under 16, no financial disputes and no mental illness. All other divorces, defended and undefended, have to be heard in the Court of Session, and so, even though you can now send in an affidavit of evidence instead of appearing in person if your divorce is undefended, your case still has to be presented in court by an advocate or counsel (a barrister). Advocates can only be appointed by Edinburgh solicitors, so if your solicitor doesn't practise in Edinburgh, he/she must pass all your papers on to one who does, who will then pass them on to an advocate who will then draw up your summons, based on your statement and the statements of your witnesses. It will also include your proposals for custody of the children, 'periodic allowance' (maintenance), or a 'capital sum' (lump sum) and 'aliment' (maintenance for the children). A copy will then be sent to your wife who has fourteen days in which to decide whether she will defend it or not.

Once she has made her decision, your solicitor will apply for a 'proof' – a court hearing – and if she is going to defend it, you will have to appear in court to give evidence. If she isn't going to defend it, then you can swear an 'affidavit of evidence', which will be presented in court by your advocate.

The children's future, and money matters are settled at the same hearing. If you and your wife can't agree about the children's future, the court will ask for an affidavit from an independent person – a social worker, or a junior advocate with no specialist knowledge of children, not a divorce court welfare officer, since they don't exist in Scotland.

The court will award custody (which embraces care and control, too) to one parent – usually to the mother – since there is no such thing as joint custody in Scottish law. If your wife has custody, then she has the right to make all the decisions about the children's future – including changing their names or emigrating without any reference to you, although you do have the right to go back to court if you disagree with what she intends to do.

As far as money is concerned, if you don't pay the 'periodic allowance' as ordered, the courts can't register the order, as they can in England and Wales, but they can order an 'arrestment of pay', the equivalent of 'attachment of earnings', and prevent you from selling your house or any other property, if it can be shown that you were 'wholly or partially' intending to avoid paying your wife. You can only be sent to prison for non-payment of 'aliment' (maintenance for your children).

The order for 'periodic allowance' will stay in force until your ex-wife either remarries or dies. If you die, and leave any money, then your estate has to go on paying her, which obviously puts a great strain on second marriages.

'Aliment' continues, regardless of remarriages or your death, until the children are sixteen or capable of earning your own living.

There is no decree nisi in Scotland. Once the judge pronounces your decree, it becomes absolute at once, though your wife has twenty-one days in which to appeal, so it's better not to remarry until that time has elapsed.

As far as legal aid is concerned, you can apply for it if your divorced, defended or undefended, is going to be heard at the Court of Session because you must have an advocate to represent you. The new 'postal' divorce does *not* involve a court hearing, so legal aid is not available.

Northern Ireland

The divorce laws in Northern Ireland are very similar now to those in England and Wales, with only a few procedural differences. Since 1981, undefended divorces can be heard in the divorce (county) courts, though defended divorces are still heard only in the High Court in Belfast. There is no special procedure in Northern Ireland, so if you are petitioning, you have to appear in court and give your evidence in person. Legal aid is available for all divorces.

The other major difference, if you have children, is that the court will ask for a welfare report in every case, and conciliation is compulsory, built into the system. That provision is now fully implemented, but some people involved professionally in divorce feel it comes far too late in the process to be of much value.

Useful organisations

Marriage Guidance
Look in your local phone book or contact
National Marriage Guidance Council,
Little Church Street,
Rugby — Tel: Rugby 73241

Scottish Marriage Guidance Council
58, Palmerston Place,
Edinburgh EH 12 5AZ — Tel: 031-225 5006

Northern Ireland Marriage Guidance Council
76, Dublin Road,
Belfast — Tel: Belfast 223454

Catholic Marriage Advisory Council
England and Wales
15, Lansdowne Road,
London W. 11 — Tel: 727 0141

Scotland
18, Park Circus,
Glasgow G3 6BE — Tel: 041-332 4914

Northern Ireland
4, Corrys Square
Newry — Tel: Newry 3577

Jewish Marriage Education Council
529b, Finchley Road,
London N.W. 3 — Tel: 01-794 5222

National Council for the Divorced and Separated
Look in your local phone book or write to
13, High Street,
Little Shelford,
Cambridge

Divorce Conciliation and Advisory Service
38, Ebury Street,
London S.W. 1 W 0LU — Tel: 01-730 2422

Institute of Marital Studies
Tavistock Clinic,
120, Belsize Lane,
London N.W. 3 Tel: 01-435 7111

Conciliation
At the time of writing, there are conciliation services in Barnet, Herts; Bristol: Bromley, Kent; Middlesbrough, Cleveland; Coventry; Dorking; Leeds, Luton; Newham, east London; Wells, Somerset; Sunderland; Swindon. There were also services in the pipeline in Newcastle and Richmond-upon-Thames, and there will almost certainly be more, so check with your local Citizen's Advice Bureau, or even divorce court to see if there is one starting in your area.

Citizen's Advice Bureau
Look in your local phone book, ask at the local library, or contact
England & Wales
National Association of Citizen's Advice Bureaux
110, Drury Lane,
London W.C. 2 Tel: 01-836 9231

Scotland
12, Queen Street,
Edinburgh 2 Tel: 031-225 5323

Northern Ireland,
2, Annadale Avenue,
Belfast 7 Tel: Belfast 640011

Families Need Fathers
Ask your local Citizen's Advice Bureau for the nearest branch or contact
Families Need Fathers,
37, Carden Road,
London S.E. 15 Tel: 01-639 5362

Campaign for Justice in Divorce
PO BOX 164
Aylesbury,
Bucks HP 17 8XQ Tel: 0296-748974

Gingerbread
Ask your local Citizen's Advice Bureau, look in the phone book or contact
Gingerbread
(England and Wales)
35, Wellington Street,
London W.C. 2 Tel: 01-240 0953

(Scotland)
39, Hope Street,
Glasgow 3 Tel: 041-248 6840

Northern Ireland
171, University Street,
Belfast 7 Tel: 0232 249 358

National Council for One Parent Families
England and Wales
255, Kentish Town Road,
London N.W. 5 Tel: 01-267 1361

Scotland
44, Albany Street,
Edinburgh EH 1 3QR Tel: 031-556 3899

Child Poverty Action Group (for help with welfare rights queries)
1 Macklin Street,
London W.C. 2 Tel: 01-405 5942/4517

National Federation of Solo Clubs
Room 8,
Ruskin Chambers,
191, Corporation Street,
Birmingham 4 Tel: 021-236 2879

Singlehanded Ltd,
Thorne House,
Hankham Place,
Stone Cross,
Pevensey, E. Sussex Tel: Eastbourne 767507

Family Rights Group
6-9 Manor Gardens,
Holloway Road,
London N7 Tel: 01-272 6308/4231

Further reading

Divorce and the law

Getting a Divorce (Consumer Association)
Acting in Person: How to Obtain an Undefended Divorce (Oyez Publishing)
A Guide to Scots Law, Richard Keith & George Clark (Johnston & Bacon)

Children
Surviving the Breakup, Judith Wallerstein and Joan Kelly (Grant McIntyre)
Divorce and your Children, Anne Hooper (George Allen & Unwin)
Saturday Parent, Peter Rowlands (George Allen & Unwin)

For children
Divorce can happen to the nicest people, Peter Mayle (W. H. Allen)
I have two homes, Althea Brouthwaite (Dinosaur Publications)

For teenagers
It's not the end of the world, Judy Blume (Pan Books)

Money
Divorce and Your Money, W. M. Harper (George Allen & Unwin)

Emotions
I'm Leaving, Bente and Gunnar Oberg (Jill Norman and Hobhouse)

Going It Alone
One Parent Families, Diana Davenport (Pan Books)

Marrying again
The Half Parent, Brenda Maddox (Andre Deutsch)
How to survive as a Second Wife, Maggie Drummond (Robson Books)
Making a Go of It, Jacqueline Burgoyne & David Clark

Index